SPY SUB

SPY SUB

A TOP SECRET
MISSION TO THE
BOTTOM OF THE PACIFIC

Roger C. Dunham

NAVAL INSTITUTE PRESS
Annapolis, Maryland

Dunham, Roger C., 1944–

    Spy Sub: A top secret mission to the bottom of the Pacific / Roger C. Dunham.

        p.   cm.

    Includes bibliographical references and index.

    ISBN 1-55750-178-5   (cloth: alk. paper)

    1. Intelligence service–United States. 2. United States. Navy–Submarine forces. 3. Soviet Union. Voenno-Morskoĭ Flot–Submarine forces. 4. Submarine disasters–Soviet Union. I. Title.

VB231.U54D86   1996

359.9'33'0973–dc20   96-10576

Printed in the United States of America on acid-free paper ∞

03 02 01 00 99 98 97 96   9 8 7

_To the men, on patrol beneath the seas,
who serve our country in the
United States Submarine Service_

CONTENTS

ACKNOWLEDGMENTS

THE CONFIDENTIAL NATURE OF THIS PROJECT prevents credit to many people who are well deserving of tribute for their assistance. I received encouragement and help from several of my shipmates, and I am thankful for invaluable assistance from Chief Warrant Officer Sandy Harless, USN (Ret.); Captain C. E. Moore, USN (Ret.); and Senior Chief Petty Officer Gary Patterson, USN (Ret.). Sandy Munroe and Val Muth provided encouragement and helpful information used in developing the story. John P. Craven, Ph.D., provided details that were useful in many ways, and four individuals working with the Department of Defense, whose identities must remain unknown, provided valuable assistance and guidance. The long hours of editing by my wife, Keiko, helped me to resolve many technical matters. I also greatly appreciate the editorial assistance of Terry Belanger.

Richard Whiston, JD, provided generous assistance and availability during the challenges of manuscript development. The recounting of personal experiences by Max Brown, senior vice president, CaliforniaCare Health Plans, was helpful to certain important aspects of the manuscript. Joseph Lord and Alvina Lord gave me invaluable access to military channels for which I will always be appreciative. Historian Sue Lemmon, Mare Island Naval Shipyard; David Stumpf, Ph.D.; and FTB1(SS) Don Merrigan, USN (Ret.), provided encouragement and valuable technical assistance.

I am especially thankful to the men who served with me on board our submarine during the difficult times of the late 1960s: from "Mathews," who almost lost it all, to "Lane," who paid far too high a price, and from the men who taught me nuclear operations to those who learned them from me. These were the people who believed in our mission and made it successful. Like those currently dedicating their lives to our country, these men were the finest of our society. They brought a high degree of credit to the Submarine Service of the U.S. Navy. That I was privileged to serve as their shipmate was a great honor.

SPY SUB

This is a true story.

The mission of the USS *Viperfish* (not the submarine's real name) was top secret.

Technical modifications are employed to protect the intelligence interests of the U.S. Navy Submarine Service. The names of the crew are changed to preserve the privacy of the brave men who served in this elite branch of the Navy during the events chronicled in this story.

PROLOGUE

THE LADY HAD BECOME a widow long before her time.

Dressed in elegant attire appropriate for the formal gathering of United States and Russian government officials, she had been invited to the affair only because of the military stature of her late husband. This would be her last encounter with these officials; she knew there were no further ties between herself and those who planned such events.

She spotted the cluster of American naval officers standing at the far side of the room. Their dark uniforms were resplendent with gold braid that gave testimony to their rank. As she slowly approached them, their hushed conversation abruptly died and their expressions showed the polite and detached affect of diplomatic propriety. They turned to accommodate her presence, and she hesitated briefly before speaking.

Only a year before, her question would have been unthinkable, but improved relations and eased tensions between the two governments offered her promise of learning the truth.

Looking into their eyes as if searching for an answer, she took a deep breath before she spoke. Her English was nearly perfect, with little dialect to reveal her origin within the vast reaches of the former Soviet Union.

"Could you tell me what has happened to my husband?" The simple question seemed to burn through the air with a raging intensity. Her tone reflected the strength of feelings contained for many years.

"Your husband?" the tallest officer said after a pause. He was polite and showed the proper degree of interest.

"He was the captain of a submarine," she answered, her voice now carrying a trace of pride. "He was the commanding officer of the Soviet submarine PL–751, in the Pacific Ocean."

"The PL–751?" another officer asked, his voice mildly curious.

"You people called it an Echo submarine. My husband and the PL–751 never returned to Vladivostok."

Their expressions did not change, and they showed no indication of any knowledge about the matter placed before them. As each looked to another for an answer, the firm voice of the older man on the left answered for them all.

"I am sorry, but we do not know about this submarine or about your husband."

Gazing across the room, the officer saw several tuxedoed men standing near the hors d'oeuvres table. He gestured with his drink in their direction.

"Perhaps if you speak to the American Consulate, they will be able to assist you."

The officer noticed her eyes beginning to redden and a look of despair on her face. "I am truly sorry," he repeated with genuine feeling as she turned and walked away.

REPORTING ON BOARD

IN MOSCOW ON THE COLD morning of 29 March 1966, the Twenty-Third Congress of the Soviet Communist Party convened at the Kremlin for the first time since the death of Nikita S. Khrushchev. In his inaugural speech before the five thousand delegates of the Communist Party's supreme ratifying body, First Secretary Leonid I. Brezhnev called for world Communist unity as he acknowledged the rapidly deteriorating relations with the United States. He protested the "bloody war by the United States against the people of South Vietnam" and called upon the Soviet military forces to continue their achievements in science and technology.

The delegates reviewed the Soviet report on military power that underscored the increasing size of their armed forces, including the Red Navy's impressive submarine fleet. They affirmed the strategy of maintaining 400 nuclear and conventional submarines in four major flotillas around the world, and they agreed to continue building their submarine fleet by 10 percent each year. The Pacific Fleet, second in size only to the massive Northern Fleet, contained 105 Soviet submarines. Many of these were of the lethal nuclear missile–carrying "E" (Echo) class that regularly patrolled the ocean waters east of Kamchatka Peninsula.

In contrast to this massive Soviet armada of submarine military power, the United States Navy possessed only 70 nuclear submarines; 41 of these vessels were designed to fire nuclear missiles and most of the others were fast–attack hunter/killer submarines. One of them, however, differed from all other submarines throughout the world.

In the spring of 1966 at the Pearl Harbor Naval Shipyard near Honolulu, Hawaii, civilian shipyard workers finished a year of intense refitting on board the nuclear submarine USS *Viperfish* (SSN 655). As the Twenty-Third Congress of the Soviet Communist Party adjourned its meeting on 8 April 1966, the U.S. Navy completed the process of gathering together a volunteer crew of 120 men to serve on board the *Viperfish*. This crew of submariners, civilian scientists, and nuclear systems operators began one of the most remarkable top secret military operations in the history of the United States.

The code name of this special mission was Operation Hammerclaw.

▼

THERE WAS NO WAY for me to know that the nuclear submarine *Viperfish* was a spy ship when I received my orders to report for sea duty.

The terse sentences on the order sheet arrived on a miserable day, a New London kind of day. Freezing winter winds blasted across the Connecticut submarine base, and the driving rain brought torture to anyone who dared to go outside. The drab buildings of the civilian city across the gray Thames River looked like dirty blocks of clay stacked along the water's edge. They seemed to fit perfectly with the dismal weather and the depressing area that must have been filled with people wanting to escape somewhere–anywhere. As a native Southern Californian who had just completed three years of submarine and nuclear reactor training, I not only craved a warmer world but I was also eager to begin the real work of running a reactor on a submarine at sea.

I had turned in my "dream sheet" weeks before. Created to give direction to the complex process of assigning personnel to duty stations, the dream sheet at least gives the illusion that the Navy tries to match each sailor's desired location with the available slots throughout the world. I had "wished" for the USS *Kamehameha*, a Polaris submarine based in Guam and skippered by someone I had known before joining the Navy. The island of Guam appealed to me because of its warm water and proximity to Hawaii, in addition to the fact that it was as far away as I could get from the submarine base at New London.

I paced back and forth within the protective interior of the musty barracks and studied the printed sheet of orders before me. The words were tiny, and I found it remarkable that such small words contained information that defined my future for the next three years: "You will report to the commanding officer of the USS *Viperfish* SSN 655 at Pearl Harbor, Hawaii."

"The *Viperfish*?" I asked into the empty barracks. "What kind of a ship is the *Viperfish*?"

Studying the orders, I searched for any kind of clue to define the vessel. She was a fast–attack nuclear submarine; the SSN (submersible ship, nuclear) before her hull number 655 left no doubt about that. Clearly, however, the Polaris option was out. The *Viperfish* was in Hawaii, the land of beautiful women and the aloha spirit, the land of warmth and excellent surf, the land that–compared with New London–was close to heaven. I scanned the order sheet again for clues about the future mission of the submarine.

To my delight, my bespectacled machinist mate friend in submarine school, Jim McGinn, was also assigned to the *Viperfish*. Looking more like a scientist than a sailor with his wispy red hair and round glasses, Jim projected a deservedly scholarly image. He excitedly popped through the barracks door that afternoon, as he waved his orders, and asked me if I knew anything about this thing called the *Viperfish*.

"I heard we're the only guys from our class to get this boat.* It must be some kind of a fast-attack," I said, offering my best educated guess. We had just completed hundreds of lectures in submarine school, and we knew there were two primary types of nuclear submarines. The majority were the SSNs, the sleek, high-performance fast-attack submarines that engaged in war games of seeking and tracking enemy submarines on the high seas. The others were the "boomers," big, slow submarines, such as the *Kamehameha*, that functioned as submergible strategic ballistic missile launching platforms. Because the *Viperfish* did not carry the SSBN designation of a boomer, she had to be one of the Navy's hot fast-attack submarines.

"But why doesn't anybody know anything about the boat?" Jim asked. "They know about all the other fast-attacks. I've asked everybody.... The *Viperfish* is like some kind of a mystery submarine."

"Probably because she's one of the newer ones," I said, "and her home port is at Pearl Harbor, on the other side of the world."

Jim smiled and looked at the cold world outside the barracks window. "Thank God for that, in warm and beautiful Hawaii."

Cursing the bone-chilling wind and rain, we crossed the base to the military library and pulled out the most recent edition of *Jane's Fighting Ships* and searched for the *Viperfish*. We first discovered that she used to be designated a guided Regulus missile-firing submarine. The range of the Regulus I missiles was five hundred miles, far below the thousand-plus range of the more modern Polaris missiles, although this range would be improved by the larger Regulus II missiles to one thousand miles. Each Regulus missile had stubby wings on either side of a fuselage carrying a jet engine

* The term "boat" is generally used to denote a small vessel that can be hoisted on board a ship. Early submarines were small enough to fulfill this definition. The camaraderie of the first "boat sailors" and their pride in serving on board such unique vessels resulted in this term remaining in common use among submariners. The official U.S. Navy definition of a submarine is a ship, but submarine sailors, in accordance with tradition, continue to call their vessel a boat.

that powered it to the target. When properly prepared in a time of war, its 3,000–pound nuclear warhead would then detonate at the appropriate time.

Jim continued to study *Jane's* information and search for more clues about our submarine. "What class is the *Viperfish?*" he asked, referring to the general class that often identifies the mission of a naval vessel. When we found she was in the *Viperfish* class, we began to feel depressed.

We both looked at the picture of the submarine and scanned the story. The *Viperfish* was definitely not a sleek vessel by any standard. She was commissioned in 1960 at Mare Island Naval Shipyard, with strange bulges and an unusual stretched–out segment in the front half of the hull, presumably to provide a stable launching platform for the five guided missiles previously stored in a hangar compartment within her bow. She was clearly not designed for speed, with a maximum submerged velocity of only twenty-five knots (compared with the forty–plus knots of most fast-attack submarines). Her superstructure was flanked with long rows of ugly-looking holes (limber holes or flood ports) along both sides, designed to allow seawater to enter the external shell of her superstructure during submerging operations.

McGinn continued to read the description. "The *Viperfish* was originally intended to be a diesel submarine," he said, "but at the last minute, they changed their mind."

"So they thought it might run better on nukie power," I said, "not having to run to the surface to pull in air for charging the batteries or running the diesel engine. Since I am a reactor operator, it is good that she has a nuclear reactor. Now what does she do?"

We hunched over the book. "Nothing else here," Jim said. "Whatever she does, the *Viperfish* is a regular SSN, sort of. When they took off the missiles, they got rid of the G designation previously signifying that she carried guided missiles."

I looked back at my orders. A tiny box at the corner of the sheet was labeled: "Purpose of Transfer." Within the box were the cryptic words, "For duty (sea)."

What we did not know at the time was that the *Viperfish* had been further redesignated as an oceanographic research vessel during the SALT (Strategic Arms Limitations Treaty) talks. The fact that she carried a substantial firepower of live torpedoes did not change the benign research vessel designation; therefore, she escaped being counted as a nuclear fast–attack warship for the purposes of the treaty. At that moment, however, she appeared to be some kind of a weird fast–attack submarine that carried no missiles.

I was becoming confused. "So she's a slow–attack submersible ship, nuclear–"

"Called the *Viperfish*...even the name is strange for an attack submarine. What the hell is a viperfish?"

We looked up the creature in the dictionary and found nothing. An encyclopedia also did not consider the animal worth mentioning, so we finally turned to a dusty fish book with faded color photographs of sea life.

"Here it is!" Jim said, pointing at a picture of a thick black fish with a huge mouth. "It's a deep–ocean fish with a hinged jaw and photophores that create a beacon of light..."

"It eats dead fish, grabbing them whole as they sink to the depths below," I added, studying the picture showing a single blue eye located above a glowing red streak.

"Viperfish. Couldn't they come up with a better name?"

"Ugly fish, ugly submarine, eats dead debris."

"With a huge glowing mouth. What are we getting ourselves into?"

No matter how we tried to embellish the *Viperfish*, it did not look like a submarine that would ever do anything impressive. She was slow and ugly, and she had a strange name. We trudged back to our barracks and listened in silence to the other men talking excitedly about their assignments on board such vessels as the *Dragonfish*, *Nautilus*, and *Scorpion*.

A couple of days later, McGinn and I left New London to spend time with our families before the final trip to Hawaii. When my friends in California asked about my submarine assignment, I could not avoid telling them. "Although the details are currently top secret," I said, with the secretive air of someone having insider classified information, "the *Viperfish* is one of those SSN fast–attack nuclear submarines equipped with state–of–the–art firing power. Furthermore, it is jammed with unique experimental military fire–power, the only one of her class in the world.

"No further information can be revealed at this time," I added in the hushed voice of somebody describing a CIA operation and left the rest to each person's imagination. In other words: "Don't ask any more questions, because nothing more can be revealed–it is all secret."

The conversations always ended with just the right amount of admiration and respect. For a twenty–one–year–old man ready to travel around the world in a submarine that was already an enigma, I could not have asked for more.

I flew to Hawaii on a civilian airliner contracted to the military at Travis Air Force Base in Northern California. The aircraft was packed with soldiers en route to Vietnam, and the atmosphere was filled with their gloom. The conflict in Southeast Asia was undergoing a rapid escalation at that time, and the depressed mood of the soldiers left little doubt about the fate they perceived at the end of their flight. The burly master sergeant sitting next to me looked miserable and said almost nothing throughout the entire trip.

When the plane landed at Honolulu, the sergeant just stared out the window at the clusters of vacationing tourists disembarking from nearby aircraft. As the plane doors opened, the sound of Hawaiian music entered the cabin, the fragrance of *Plumeria* blossoms floated through the air, and the lucky few of us assigned to Hawaii could not get off the plane fast enough. Jim arrived in Hawaii on a different day, but his flight carried a similar sad group of men. The memory of the unfortunate soldiers on that flight stayed with me during the tough times of the *Viperfish's* submerged operations and somehow made my work seem easier by comparison.

I called Pearl Harbor from the airport and was quickly connected to the *Viperfish*.

"USS *Viperfish*, Petty Officer Kanen speaking," the young voice
fired out. "May I help you, sir?"

Thirty minutes later, a chief petty officer from the *Viperfish*
jumped out of a car, asked my name, and firmly pumped my
hand.

"Welcome to Hawaii, Dunham, I'm Paul Mathews, from the
Viperfish–you're one of the new nukes, aren't you?" He was in his
middle thirties, I guessed, a strong–looking man of average height
and weight, and full of enthusiasm when I told him that I was a
reactor operator ready to report on board.

"Throw your seabag in the back of the car," he said with a smile,
"and we're on our way to Pearl. I'll give you a ride even though
you are a goddamn nuke."

As we drove down Kamehameha Highway under the blue sky
and brilliant tropical sunlight, Chief Mathews told me more
about the *Viperfish*. He confirmed that the submarine had been
designed to launch Regulus missiles, each equipped with a large
nuclear warhead and fired from a rail launching system on the
topside deck of the *Viperfish*. He told me that, during the past few
years, the *Viperfish* had made several deployments to the western
Pacific Ocean with nuclear missiles stored inside the cavernous
hangar compartment in the front half of the submarine. During
this time, she was the front line nuclear deterrent force for the
United States.

The *Viperfish* had made a total of thirty–two test firings of
Regulus missiles at sea. Each shot required the crew to surface,
open a large door (christened the "bat cave" by the crew), roll a
Regulus missile out of the hangar and onto its track, establish
radio contact with the guiding system of a nearby American jet,
and then finally fire the thing into the sky. The entire operation
took about twenty minutes. Immediately afterward, the crew
rapidly closed the bat cave and rigged the boat to dive so that, as
quickly as possible, the *Viperfish* could disappear beneath the sur-

face. The Regulus system provided nuclear protection prior to development of the Polaris missile program and construction of the first Polaris submarine, the USS *George Washington* (SSBN 598).

"With the Polaris missile system now going ahead full steam, the *Viperfish* isn't involved with Regulus missiles, right?" I asked Chief Mathews the obvious as we entered Pearl Harbor's main gate.

"Right," he answered. "They unloaded the missiles and changed her back to SSN." There was a period of silence, and I waited for him to continue.

Finally, feeling stupid, I blurted out, "Okay, what does the *Viperfish* do now, Chief?"

He hesitated, then began speaking in slow, measured tones. "Although her mission is secret, she has been redesigned to perform activities that you will find extraordinary. Because of these changes, there are now three crews on board the boat. There is the nuclear crew, composed of goddamn nukes like yourself, and the others who keep the reactor on the line and the steam in the engine room."

After turning left past the main gate, we were moving in the opposite direction from the arrows pointing to the submarine base.

"And then there is the forward crew, the men who *really* run the boat," he said. "They are occasionally called the forward pukes by the nukes–our shipmates to the rear. The non-nukes run the ballast control systems, the diving station, navigation, sonar, fire control–"

"I understand all that, Chief," I interrupted. "And the *third* crew?"

He took a deep breath, stared straight ahead, and softly said, "The third crew is for the Special Project."

We turned right, drove down Avenue D and into the naval shipyard. "What kind of special project, Chief?" I asked, sensing that I was going to learn little.

"You'll find out all about that from your security briefing, Dunham. All you need to know for now is that we are developing a combined civilian and military project, a cooperative effort, so to speak, that expands the capabilities of the *Viperfish*."

Although the prospect of civilians being assigned to a nuclear warship seemed unusual and even a little unsettling, it was apparent that the chief was not going to say anything more on the subject. We made a right turn off South Avenue to 7th Street, where a cluster of towering shipyard cranes came into sight. Mathews began talking about cranes as we approached the dry dock area. He said that the largest cranes were of the "hammer–head" style, as unique to Pearl Harbor as the Arizona Memorial.

The *Viperfish* was not moored at the Southeast Loch submarine base with the other submarines. The *Viperfish* wasn't even in the water. Mathews parked the car, and we walked in the direction of the biggest dry dock, looming like a gigantic rectangular hole ahead of us. I stopped at the edge of the massive concrete chamber and stared down at the submarine that was to be my new home for the next three years.

2

PREPARATION FOR SEA

SINCE THE EARLY 1960S, the waters off the eastern coast of the Kamchatka Peninsula have been closely monitored by United States surveillance systems that acoustically track submarines as they approach and depart the naval bases at Vladivostok and Petropavlovsk. One of the most comprehensive of these systems is the passive hydrophone array, known by the Department of Defense as the sound surveillance system (code–named SOSUS), capable of accurately identifying the positions of ships at sea. Installed at a cost of $16 billion and stretching for thirty thousand miles, the SOSUS microphones were arranged in a highly classi-fied manner throughout the Atlantic and Pacific oceans for the primary purpose of detecting Soviet missile–carrying submarines. By 1966, this system was already in operation and quietly analyz-ing the acoustic signatures of Soviet submarines sailing from their home ports into the Pacific Ocean from the Sea of Okhotsk and the Kamchatka Peninsula.

The ocean is filled with noise spanning a wide range of fre-quencies emitted by abundant biological life-forms. From the train of sharp clicks generated by the sperm whales (often rattling thirty to forty clicks per second, they sound like a cadre of carpenters hammering simultaneously) to the growling of the fin whales, the rasping and drumming of the triggerfish, and the whistles of the killer whales, SOSUS heard them all. With regularity, the sensitive microphones of SOSUS detected the deep-throated rumbles from the screws of passing freighters mixing with the clatter of Soviet diesel submarines as they ran their engines to charge their batteries. Less commonly, SOSUS picked up the sounds of explosive charges detonated by antisubmarine aircraft and ships, along with a profusion of underwater communications, during war game activities.

Every ten or twenty years, maybe once or rarely twice in the career of a SOSUS specialist, there were the loud noises of collapsing steel and rupturing compartments as a vessel on the high seas lost her integrity and began to break apart. On these infrequent occasions, the noise continued for a minute, sometimes longer, as the ship dropped below the surface and, falling thousands of feet, broadcast her trail of progressive destruction into the sensitive microphones on the bottom of the sea. When the reverberations finally ceased and the ocean was returned to the sounds of the whales and the fish, the SOSUS analysts were left with a final epitaph to the men and the vessel that no longer existed.

▼

THE *VIPERFISH* WAS A monster of a submarine.

Stretching 350 feet from bow to stern, she was bigger than any vessel I had seen at New London. Sitting high on blocks arranged across the sunken floor of the dry dock, she looked like an ominous black trophy on display. Any sleek lines envisioned by her designers never made it to the final product. Flapperlike bow planes sticking out near her nose gave her the appearance of a 1930s submarine, the huge tumorous hump bulging out of her skin disrupted her shape, and the square limber holes along her sides looked like a colossal engineering mistake.

Torrents of water shot straight out from holes in her flanks and, arcing far into the air, fell to the concrete floor below. Workmen scurried over the various steel protrusions and sent streams of sparks across the hull as their grinders and air hammers clattered a dissonant cacophony. In the background, barely audible through the bedlam from the dry dock, curious clanging sounds announced the movements of the enormous cranes rolling across railroad tracks around the perimeter of the dry dock as their cables lowered open crates filled with men to the deck of the submarine.

"Ugly bastard, ain't she?" Mathews hollered over the noise of the chaos in front of us.

"Never seen anything like it," I called back.

"There is *nothing* like the *Viperfish* anywhere in the world."

The chief and I each donned a blue plastic hard hat from the stack near one of the cranes and climbed into an open wooden box at the side of the dry dock. After a shipyard worker signaled the crane operator, the cable over our heads snapped tight. The crane abruptly lifted us high into the air over the cavernous dry dock and then propelled us in the general direction of the *Viperfish*.

I looked down at the dark concrete far below. At the same instant, the chief yelled, "Don't look down, it's a long drop!"

We landed on the *Viperfish* deck with a jarring thud. Mathews led the way to the forward hatch—a circular hole on the surface of the deck—and down a long vertical steel ladder to the central control station.

The inside of the *Viperfish* appeared to be in a state of total disorder. As military and civilian personnel worked side by side on numerous pieces of electronic equipment, the tight compartment was buzzing with the electricity of energized circuits. I sniffed the pungent odor of diesel oil mixed with the smells of new linoleum, fresh paint, and sweat and wondered about the oxygen levels inside this tight enclosure of human activity.

The bulkheads (walls) of the compartment were covered with hundreds of red, yellow, and green lights blinking on and off like a Christmas tree. Several drawers, filled with electronic equipment, had been pulled out from the bulkhead. Wires were hanging out of them—some connected to other wires from other drawers, others poking freely into the air. Men in blue dungaree uniforms were busy working on the periscope lens assemblies at the ends of long shafts extending down from the overhead spaces. Others were cursing and struggling with the steering wheels at the diving station, where a pair of cushioned chairs had been bolted. Later, I learned that the chairs were for the planesman and helmsman as they controlled the depth, course, and trim angle of the submarine.

The men in front of us occasionally glanced in my direction. I felt awkward in my clean white uniform. Standing next to Chief Mathews at the bottom of the ladder, I was moving my head back and forth, with my eyes wide open in wonder. I knew that I presented the unmistakable appearance of a rookie.

A couple of the men nodded a greeting to us as the chief guided me out of the control center and up a passageway to the yeoman's office. I signed a stack of papers filled with legal jargon; the yeoman mumbled something about gamma rays and handed me a clip-on radiation film badge. We moved forward again to the captain's stateroom. Mathews rapped on the door, and the commanding officer of the *Viperfish* promptly invited us into his cramped quarters.

Capt. Stuart Gillon was a short man with a worried expression on his face. He looked like the burdens of the world were weighing heavily on him. He was of small frame and spoke with a soft voice that was hard to hear. My first thought was that this could not possibly be the captain of a nuclear warship. The captain should look more like a skipper, I thought—tall, strong voice, square jaw, and the other features that I considered to be requisites for such an important position.

And then I noticed the intensity of the man's eyes. They reflected a perceptive intelligence as he studied me closely, sizing me up, listening to what I said, and taking measure of the newest enlisted man who would, someday, run his boat's nuclear reactor. Although his voice was kindly, his words were concise and his thinking tightly organized. He displayed intense concentration and focus of thoughts. Quietly, he began to tell me about future activities on the *Viperfish* and encouraged me to begin qualifications promptly because the mission mandated a fully qualified crew.

"We're coming out of dry dock in a couple of months," he said, "and we'll be conducting sea trials, followed by a shakedown cruise to Seattle and San Francisco. We'll be testing the Fish soon thereafter, and, by that time, you should be standing watches at the reactor control panel. Do you think you can handle all that?"

"Yes, sir," I answered briskly, wondering what fish he was referring to. *Jane's Fighting Ships* didn't mention anything about a fish, and submarine school hadn't described fish equipment on any submarines in the fleet. Before I had the chance to ask questions, he told me how pleased he was to have me on board and dismissed me with a quick nod to Chief Mathews.

"You'll find out about the Fish when you start qualifications," Mathews said after we left the captain's stateroom and headed aft. "The next stop is the engine room, where you'll have the pleasure of meeting Bruce."

We climbed through the thick oval doors into a confining corridor leading to the engine room. Mathews paused and called back to me, "This is the reactor tunnel and the nuclear reactor is directly below you. When we're at sea and the reactor is running, you'll want to move through this area pretty fast." I looked down at my feet and discovered a large circular ring carved in the floor, presumably "ground zero." The constricted area around me was jammed with valves and pipes, and several signs displayed the nuclear symbol that warned of radiation. As I ducked my 6'2" frame around various steel obstructions protruding from the tunnel's overhead, we continued to move aft until we reached the last watertight door and the engine room. The room was hot and filled with the suffocating odor of burning diesel fuel. Surrounded by insulated pipes, gauges, valves, and circuit breakers, I came face to face with the man who was in charge of the *Viperfish's* nuclear reactor operators.

"Bruce, this is Dunham, fresh from New London, your new reactor operator," Mathews said. Bruce Rossi was a tough, powerful man with a burr haircut and coal-black eyes that scrutinized me closely. He barked a loud greeting and gave me a tight smile. With his heavily muscled right hand, he reached out and crushed my hand.

"Reactor operator *trainee*, Paul. Glad you're here, Dunham," he growled.

"Happy to be on board, Bruce," I replied. His pulsating jaw muscles suggested a significant measure of controlled anger.

He stared at me. "Let me get right to the issue at hand because there's a lot of work to be done," he said. "The *Viperfish* is powered by a complex water-cooled S3W nuclear reactor, and our division requires three ROs [reactor operators] qualified to control the system. Two of the ROs will be finishing their tour of duty and will be leaving the boat after the sea trials and our shakedown run. The *Viperfish* will, therefore, need replacement reactor operators. You are one of the replacements, and Petty Officer Richard Daniels will be the second replacement when he arrives in the next few days. Both of you are going to work your tails off to learn every system in the engine room and on the *Viperfish*. You need to become qualified on this boat. Fall behind on the qualifications schedule, and you will find yourself on the dink list."

Mathews smiled and turned to leave. "Don't be too hard on the guy, Bruce," he said over his shoulder. "This is his first boat."

"The dink list?" I asked Bruce.

Rossi's face looked tougher. "The delinquent list," he said. "It's updated every day, posted in the control center near the periscope station, and in plain sight for everyone to see. If you fall behind on qualifications, you will land on the dink list, you will remain on board the *Viperfish*, and your liberty will be curtailed. That means you can't leave the boat and you don't visit Waikiki. You will eat here and sleep here until you get caught up. I don't want any of my trainees on the goddamn dink list, and I don't want any of my qualified ROs standing goddamn port and starboard watches."

An old chief told me, a long time ago, that the Submarine Service is unique because the men are pleasant and they get along so well together–I decided that chief had never met Bruce Rossi. Although the dink list program sounded almost like a prison system, I figured it would never become a threat to me; Rossi looked like he would kill, with his own bare hands, anybody who dared to come close to getting on the dink list.

I nodded to Bruce that I understood and then glanced at the engine–room equipment around us. There were thousands of pipes, valves, and large pieces of powerful–looking steel machinery jammed into every available space. To become qualified, I knew I would have to know where each pipe went, what each valve controlled, and how every piece of machinery worked.

I turned back to Bruce. "Port and starboard watches refers to–?" I asked, trying to remain polite.

His faded blue dungaree shirt tightened across his chest as his muscles tensed with annoyance.

"Six hours on watch, six hours off, six on, six off, over and over again, week after week, month after month" he growled. "Somebody has to control the nuclear reactor, Dunham, and it can't be a man who isn't qualified. Furthermore, when we leave on our mission, the captain doesn't want his boat filled with non–qual pukes. If you and Daniels are too slow to get there and we end up with only two qualified reactor operators, they are going to be standing port and starboard watches and I am going to be pissed. Get yourself checked into the submarine barracks, pick up your qualification card from the chief of the boat, and start your quals–today. I want those systems signed off; I want you to be well on your way to becoming an RO before the *Viperfish* leaves the dry dock."

For the next several weeks, I chased back and forth throughout the boat and learned system after system as if my life depended on it. I quickly discovered that trying to learn about the complex equipment in the engineering spaces of a submarine in dry dock was nearly impossible. Because of the disassembled state of the engine room, I found it difficult just to walk around the passage-ways, much less to learn anything about the equipment. Parts of motors, pumps, and circuits were strewn everywhere. Just moving across the decking area required great care to avoid stepping on some vital component.

Although I had just completed several years of rigorous nuclear training, I found it even more difficult to figure out the operation of a submarine system that was partially in pieces. Also, the most critical parts always seemed to be missing. I searched through the thick *Reactor Plant Manual* for pictures of each system that I needed to learn, but *finding* the essential components in the maze of pipes and meters was a daunting challenge. Often, I had to locate a qualified crew member to tell me what I had missed.

When the qualified man was finished with his instructions, it was quiz time: Did I know everything there was to know about the system? If not, "Start over again, you non–qual puke, and *pay attention* this time." If the quiz went well, the system was signed off, there was one less thing to learn, and I was one tiny notch farther along the tortuous pathway toward submarine qualifications.

The electricity was always turned off when equipment was dis-assembled. To lessen the risk of accidentally energizing a circuit during repair work, red tags were placed all over the circuit breaker and not removed until it was demonstrated that no dan-ger of electric shock or other problems existed. When it was time to turn on the electricity, however, I discovered that things often went very wrong.

"Okay, remove the red tags and turn it on!" the electrician hollered down the passageway to the man standing next to the tagged circuit breaker when a repair was completed.

"Okay, here it goes!" the man hollered back as he removed the red tags and placed his hand on the breaker.

The electrician threw the switch, and there was a brilliant elec-trical flash with the "clap" noise of current flowing through the circuit breaker. The men standing around the equipment watched closely as the current raced through repaired circuits and brought the device to life. When equipment did not function properly, which seemed to happen with amazing regularity, a moment of silence was followed by furious arm waving and screaming: "Turn if off! Turn it off! Turn it off!"

That scenario was followed by a torrent of cursing, which often included phrases unique to the submarine service and words that I had never heard before. When the cursing was over, the circuit breaker was locked open again and the painful process of repairing equipment started again.

Although the crew of the *Viperfish* appeared to be a single unified group of men, I soon discovered that it was actually an accumulation of 120 volunteers for submarine duty who were in a state of flux. Someone was always coming in or going out. The men on board the boat at any time were significantly different from those who had been there one year before and those who would be there a couple of years later. Members of the crew reported on board or left for reasons of seniority, completion of defined tours of duty, and many other factors. I did not know it at the time, but the personnel turnover was less than was usual in the Navy. Washington's BuPers (Bureau of Personnel) had worked to stabilize the crew of the *Viperfish* to a relatively fixed complement of men for this mission.

The veteran group was the core of the crew when I reported on board. These men had been qualified on all of the systems for several months or years, and several had been previously qualified on one or more other submarines before reporting to the *Viperfish*. They were the recognized pros, the men who had their dolphins.

The "dolphins," an internationally recognized pin, is worn above the breast pocket of dress uniforms. The pin depicts a pair of dolphins, on either side of a World War II submarine, guiding it to safety. The dolphins represent "qualified in submarines," a symbol that is the coveted treasure awaiting non-qual pukes struggling to learn about their submarines. Wearing the dolphins means that the individual has been granted membership in one of the most exclusive clubs in the world.

To me, the qualifications process was almost like a mandate from God: until I earned my dolphins and until the captain certified me to be qualified on all of the *Viperfish* systems, I could not belong to the club.

The men of the qualified crew on the *Viperfish* knew exactly what they were doing. They knew which valves should be shut and which should be open; they knew which electrical and mechanical systems should be on and operating and which should be in standby. The man sitting in front of the ballast control panel knew how to maintain neutral buoyancy, important for proper depth control. The men controlling the reactor systems, those high above us in the cramped cockpit of the sail, and those who would later prepare our food and tend to our medical needs were all skilled in their areas of expertise, thus allowing the crew of the *Viperfish* to function as one cohesive unit of qualified men. The confidence that the qualified men had in each other was the force behind the enduring shipmate camaraderie, the essence of life for the men serving on board the *Viperfish*.

Those who were not yet qualified in submarines were treated as if they knew nothing, regardless of their rank or intelligence. Officers often needed instruction and signatures from enlisted men, while enlisted men frequently turned to officers for information. If a man was not qualified and was on the dink list, he was at the absolute bottom of the pecking order.

The civilian scientists in the bow compartment (also called the hangar compartment) where the mysterious Fish was supposed to be, were not involved in the qualifications process, and their interaction with the crew was minimal. They were on the *Viperfish* to accomplish a mission. Clearly, they did not want to talk about their work to any of us, so we simply treated them, in a polite manner, as civilian outsiders and left them to their own work on the Special Project.

The heart of the Special Project operation was in the forward third of the submarine, in the cavernous hangar compartment that formerly contained the Regulus missiles. With no under-standing of what the project was about and with nobody inclined to say anything specific about it, I simply added Special Project to the vast number of mysteries on board the *Viperfish*.

Whenever I went through the bow compartment as I studied the location of various cables and valves, I moved past the cluster of civilians looking down into a huge hole that penetrated the decking of the compartment. Walking around the men gathered above the hole and ignoring their hushed conversations, I contin-ued forward until I either bumped into the torpedo tubes or iden-tified the location of the equipment I was studying. With the wrath of Bruce hanging over my head if I didn't move ahead with qualifications at full speed, I felt that civilian scientists looking down big holes were of little importance.

Richard Daniels reported on board within a week of my arrival, and now two potential reactor operators studied *Viperfish* tech manuals, searched for crewmen who knew the systems, and struggled to show progress with qualifications. In his early twen-ties, Richard was a tall, intelligent man with a Georgia accent. He immediately developed a respect for Bruce Rossi's grinding jaw muscles and scowling looks. Early in the qualifications process, he informed me that he had little inclination to die at the hands of Rossi, especially before getting qualified. Richard also had never been on a submarine before. Inside this gigantic steel vessel, we both felt an equal sense of anticipation as we prepared for our secret mission below the surface of the Pacific Ocean.

After a couple of weeks, Chief Mathews handed out the rack assignments to the berthing area. Located in the center of the ship, the racks (bunks) were stacked in columns of three. Each rack included a pillow, a thin mattress, a blanket stretched over cotton sheets, an air conditioning vent, a tiny neon light, and a locker under the mattress for personal belongings. Opened by pulling up on the hinged mattress support, the locker was about six inches

high and spanned the length of the bunk. Most important, there
was actually a curtain that could be pulled across the rack's opening—privacy on a submarine, a luxury previously unheard of.

My rack was far more than just a place to sleep. When we left
dry dock, it would become my sanctuary from the rest of the submarine world. I was assigned the middle rack; by lifting myself up
and squeezing sideways into the coffinlike opening and then
reaching out and pulling my curtain shut, I was suddenly
enclosed in a world of privacy that was unavailable anywhere else
on the boat. The mattress, although comfortable, was very narrow
and barely six feet long (requiring a slight bending of my knees if
I kept my neck straight). In the event of a sneeze, I had to quickly
turn my head to keep from crashing into the steel underside of
the rack above me. Otherwise, the enclosure offered most of the
comforts of a good bed at home.

The months in the shipyard passed, the qualifications continued, and the big day finally arrived when the *Viperfish* could leave
the dry dock and float to the pier at the submarine base. Floating
the submarine off the blocks in dry dock and moving her a mere
half mile across the Southeast Loch to her new berthing spot was
a remarkably complicated operation. As one of the newest men
on board, I was assigned a trainee position. I sat next to my
friend, Jim McGinn, at a watch station controlling the delivery of
steam to the turbine systems turning the screws. During the early
hours of the morning, I watched the vigorous work of the qualified crewmen bringing the reactor to an operational status, drawing steam into the engine room, and checking all of the seawater
valves. Finally, I heard Chief Mathews announce over the *Viperfish*
loudspeaker system: "Now, station the maneuvering watch! All
hands, station the maneuvering watch!"

There was a feeling of excitement as we prepared for the trans-
formation from a stationary mass of steel resting on blocks in the
center of the dry dock to a functioning submarine that would
soon be ready to go to sea. With Bruce Rossi standing nearby and
watching over all of the trainees, Jim and I gripped the throttle

wheels controlling the flow of steam to the turbines and awaited orders.

In the engine-room spaces around us, machinist mates, electronic technicians, electricians, and engineering officers took their positions in front of the panels that controlled various parts of the nuclear propulsion and turbogenerator systems. The sound of steam hissing through insulated piping added to the excitement as we waited for orders from the officer of the deck (OOD) in the control center to rotate the steam wheels and open our throttles.

The seawater of Pearl Harbor swirled into the dry dock, covered the blocks under the hull of the *Viperfish*, and rose around her superstructure. The boat finally floated as the dock filled to sea level. Squeezed into the tiny cockpit at the top of the sail (formerly called the conning tower in the older diesel boats), the captain, a junior officer, and two lookouts took their positions and prepared to call orders to the engine room over the loudspeaker communication system.

Jim turned to me at the instant that we first felt the slight movement of the submarine's hull.

"We're off the blocks," he said, excitedly. "Cheers to the forward pukes–they're doing something right."

"All ahead one third!" blared from the loudspeaker over my head, and the bell indicator clanged as the needle pointed to the ordered bell. Jim and I grabbed the wheels in front of us. Cranking them to the left, we heard the whining noises of the main propulsion turbines spooling up. We could feel the vibrations of the hull caused by the screws rotating in the water behind us. I felt a surge of excitement at being a crewman actually controlling the movements of a fleet submarine moving across Pearl Harbor.

In a nearby area called the maneuvering room, the reactor operator and electric plant operator sat rigidly upright in front of the lights and meters of their complex panels to observe any abnormalities that could shut down the reactor or trip a turbogenerator off-line. Except for the sensation of floating, there was no way to confirm that we were moving out of the dry dock or to know our direction and speed. The *Viperfish* had no windows. With the engine–room hatches all closed and clamped shut, we could see nothing as we moved across the bay. After several minutes of speculation, we tried to guess where we were from the movements of the hull, an effort that proved to be a futile waste of time.

Suddenly, the central 1MC loudspeaker system blared, "Attention to port!"

I looked at Jim. "Attention to port?" I asked.

He shrugged his shoulders. From behind us, Bruce Rossi's growling voice came to life.

"Attention to port is a call of respect," he said.

Jim and I looked appropriately confused. I glanced back at Bruce and asked, "Respect to whom, Bruce?"

"Respect for the men of the USS *Arizona*. They are off our port bow, right about now, and the men topside are giving the traditional salute to show respect as we pass by."

Jim and I felt the impact of his statement as our enthusiasm turned to somber silence. We spent the remainder of the ten-minute trip with some quiet thoughts about the men still trapped within the steel walls of their destroyed battleship, the men who never had a chance of survival during the 1941 attack on Pearl Harbor.

The sudden and urgent call through the loudspeakers from the officers on the bridge, "Back one third," gave us a clue that we were approaching our berth at the submarine base. The quick, high–pitched "Back emergency" that came shortly thereafter, immediately followed by the sound of crushing wood, gave us the best indication that we had, in a manner of speaking, arrived at the pier.

"What's that noise?" I hollered to Jim over the whining sounds of turbines and steam.

"It sounds like we just squashed a wooden rowboat against the pier," he hollered back.

Rossi gave us the answer. We had just crushed a "camel," the wooden structure attached near the pilings of the pier. Normally, a submarine gently touches the camel, so that the boat's superstructure is held away from, and not damaged by, the thick pilings. The floating camel has two functions: to protect the pier from the crushing force of a submarine and to protect the submarine from being crushed against the pier. When the camel is approached too rapidly, as the *Viperfish* had just done, the device is easily crushed. Inside the boat, the noise of splintering wood is exceedingly loud. I would hear this sound many more times during the months and years ahead when various junior officers, working on their qualifications, tried to maneuver the ungainly hulk of the *Viperfish* near a pier and took out the camels one by one.

After the reactor was shut down, I climbed up the long ladder that passed through the engine-room hatch to the topside deck. Standing on the black steel hull, I looked at the new world around me. The change of scenery from the shipyard was remarkable. Several black submarines, sitting low in the water and looking extremely sleek in comparison to the *Viperfish*, stretched out in a long row ahead and astern of us.

I could almost sense the presence of the deep Pacific Ocean, only three miles away, waiting to challenge and test us during our upcoming sea trials. Although the *Viperfish* had not yet submerged and we had crossed only a small span of calm water, this had been my first real submarine voyage, and I had actually controlled the engine-room steam during the trip. I looked at the western horizon, and I felt an excitement that we now had a functional submarine with an operating nuclear reactor. The *Viperfish* had floated without flooding, and, deep in our bow compartment, we had a mysterious Fish with miles of cable waiting to fulfill our promise for the future.

3

SEA TRIALS

DURING THE FIRST HALF of the 1960s, the Soviet Union built twenty-nine deadly submarines designed to perform one specific function: deliver high explosives and nuclear warheads from launching platforms at sea. Built in the Severodvinsk and Komsomolsk ship-yards, these submarines were deployed to improve the Soviet's ability to counter the perceived threat from Western strike carriers while simultaneously threatening American naval bases, such as shipyards, operational bases, airfields, and supply depots.

As Soviet submarines left their home port of Vladivostok, the microphones of the SOSUS array tracked them across the Sea of Japan and through the choke points at the Kuril Islands. As the SSGN submarines carrying guided missiles patrolled across the Pacific Ocean in the direction of the Hawaiian Islands and the West Coast of the United States, the Soviet Union stepped up its pattern of saber rattling and threats to compete with "sharp swords" for international military supremacy.

By summer 1966, Soviet anger at the involvement of the United States in the Vietnam conflict increased as B–52 bombers from the

U.S. Strategic Air Command began bombing enemy forces in Southeast Asia. Thousands of Americans were drafted into military service, and many participated in ground combat activities, in which U.S. Ranger battalions fought the Vietcong in actions that resulted in large numbers of casualties on both sides. The U.S. Navy became more directly involved in the combat as jets from the USS *Enterprise* and USS *Hancock* bombed North Vietnamese targets, including a variety of boats carrying supplies for the Vietcong.

The American public became increasingly aroused at the mounting U.S. casualties, and new antiwar activities began to spread throughout the United States.

WITH THE *VIPERFISH* FLOATING alongside the pier at Pearl Harbor, qualifications on her systems began to assume a brisk pace. Overhauled equipment, now reassembled, was working; electronic panels with their array of lights and meters were energized; and piping diagrams could be followed until the systems were thoroughly memorized.

The scientists working with our Special Project became known by the crew as scientists on board (SOBs). Although they were not in the Navy, there was a pecking order of sorts, including a senior SOB named Lt. Gerry Short, who seemed to direct the others. Because Lieutenant Short was not strictly a civilian, being attached to some branch of an Air Force Intelligence group, nobody was quite sure how to deal with him. We didn't salute him. He didn't wear an Air Force uniform. He didn't tell any stories about flying airplanes, and none of us ever did figure out why our Special Project required somebody from the Air Force.

Three of the crew on board the *Viperfish* worked with the Special Project. Lean and quiet Lt. Al Dobkin and the ship's photographer, a perky man named Robbie Teague, were assigned to work with the civilians under the capable but taciturn Comdr. John Spiegel. All three men remained as secretive about the Special Project as everyone else who called the *Viperfish* hangar their home. The whole collection of civilians, the two naval officers, the Air Force officer, and the enlisted Navy photographer stayed in the hangar area of the submarine most of the time, as they had when we were in dry dock, and seldom mingled with the rest of us.

At mealtime, the SOBs and other Special Project men wandered into the crew's dining area when the food was served. They ate quietly without joining in the ribald humor that characterized our dining experience. When they finished eating, they silently glided back to the hangar. The entire group seemed to be scientific engineering types, with interests selectively focused on their project.

In fact, I learned later that the remoteness of the non–Navy SOBs resulted from a degree of intimidation at being in such a foreign environment and surrounded by more than a hundred submariners. Also, their movements on board were constrained because they were physically bound by the security regulations that held them to the limits of their work with the Fish. Although they did not show much visible excitement for these reasons, I came to learn that they were proud to be serving with the *Viperfish* crew and they readily trusted us to bring them back from the submerged explorations that lay ahead.

As the qualifications work became more intense and the size of our crew expanded, Marc Birken reported on board the *Viperfish*. Marc was a veteran of the Polaris submarine USS *Daniel Boone* and a lover of sports cars and "steaming" (blowing off steam on liberty). He was aching to finish his obligation in the Navy as quickly as possible so that he could return to civilian life and teach in the trade schools of Ohio. Marc was a fun–loving man who viewed the submarine world with a "hang loose, baby" attitude. He was in love with his TR–3 convertible sports car, which regularly squealed him around Waikiki. One of the nukes, he was an electrician by training and his dolphins were the pride of his life.

The first time he passed by the reactor operator area and noticed Bruce Rossi's characteristic tense face and mean looks, he glanced sideways toward me and struggled to avoid the grin that was his trademark. We quickly became friends, and he regularly chastised me for worrying about Bruce and having too serious an attitude.

The days passed quickly at the submarine base. Working my way through one system after another, I moved beyond any threat of placement on the dink list. When confinement among the men and machinery of the *Viperfish*, day after day, became too oppressive, the sweet call of liberty in Waikiki beckoned seductively from the east. The process of going on liberty and steaming was widely regarded as the solution to an oppressed mind.

For us, steaming consisted of a high-speed departure from the *Viperfish* to the barracks, a hot shower with plenty of soap to wash off the unique odors of a submarine, the donning of civvies (civilian clothes) to disguise our military origin, and the jumping into a Cadillac taxi to roar off to Waikiki. We found that the best way to start the steaming process was at the Fort DeRussy Army Base, near the Hilton Hawaiian Village, where decent bourbon could be purchased for about thirty cents per drink. After we had consumed a proper amount of beverage, the stage was set to continue our steaming at the night spots of Waikiki.

Meeting women in Waikiki was not difficult. The surplus of dancing establishments scattered throughout the area was perfect for military men on liberty, and Marc delighted in establishing a relationship with any woman who looked even slightly interesting. On our third or fourth night of steaming, he taught me a remarkably successful way to solidify an emerging relationship with a young lady. The process started with mai tais, moonlight, and sweet Hawaiian music. It was further stimulated by Marc's gracious manner toward the ladies, mixed with his disarming sense of humor.

After several dances with an attractive woman, he leaned forward and drew her close to him. Before she knew what was coming, he innocently asked "The Question": "How would you like a tour aboard a nuclear submarine?"

This invariably resulted in a backward movement as the woman stared at him wide-eyed, blinked several times, and finally asked, "A nuclear submarine? Tonight? Are you serious? Are you in the Navy?"

He smiled and told her that he would be happy to give her a tour of his ship if she would find such a tour interesting. "It is a beautiful submarine," he said, with just the right smile and proper blend of innocence and enthusiasm. "It is called the *Viperfish* and it is an excellent warship, one of the best in the Navy. It has a nice periscope, the control room has some beautiful lights, and you would be quite safe, being on a military base and all."

The predictable result became an often-repeated routine. She smiled, having never heard such an offer from any man she had known back in Kansas City or wherever she was from, and her eyes lit up with the excitement of it all. Because the women of Waikiki rarely traveled alone, she usually asked if her girlfriend could come with her. "Of course," Marc said magnanimously, as he waved in my direction and beckoned for me to join them.

When the *Viperfish* topside watch saw our group meandering down the dark pier at 0100, we could hear the distant muttering of something relating to Jesus Christ.

After a knowing look or two and a polite salute to welcome the ladies on board, the watch greeted us and cleared the way for our late-night tour. A half hour later, after hearing the excited "ooh's" and "ah's" of our female companions, Marc and I felt like heroes for the rest of the night.

All the fun came to an end the morning the captain gathered us together on the pier in front of the *Viperfish* and told us that we were going to sea in two days. We would leave at 0800 hours, he told us, and conduct our sea trials. The purpose of the exercise, he said in his soft voice, was to test the integrity and capabilities of our submarine. It would be an envelope study of sorts, a test of our underwater limits. Although this was not a Special Project operation, the outcome of the sea trials would help to determine the success of future activities; the sea trials test was, therefore, extremely important to our mission. Once it was established that we could perform submerged activities safely and effectively, we would be ready to proceed to our West Coast shakedown cruise and, finally, to start testing the Fish.

After we completed the morning muster on the pier, I climbed down the engine-room hatch and started studying the next system on the qualifications list. My work was abruptly interrupted by Chief Paul Mathews's voice bellowing throughout the boat over the loudspeaker system.

"All men lay topside to 'sally ship'!"

Puzzled, I looked up from by book. "Do what to the ship?" I asked nobody in particular.

Bruce Rossi started climbing up the engine-room ladder to the topside deck. "Sally ship, Dunham," he barked in my direction. "Important for the calculation of metacentric height of which the center of buoyancy is a part. Get up there."

With Chief Mathews giving directions from his position in front of the submarine sail, about thirty of us lined up in a long row at the port side of the ship and crowded as close to the edge of the deck as possible. The chief looked at his wristwatch, waited a few seconds, and then hollered at the top of his lungs, "Move to the starboard side!"

We promptly rushed across the deck to the opposite side of the *Viperfish*. A few seconds later, the chief hollered again.

"Port side!"

We leaped to the port side.

"Starboard side!"

Feeling foolish, I moved with the rest of the men.

"Port!"

"Starboard!"

"Port!"

"Starboard!"

Scurrying back and forth, we paused for about six or seven seconds on each side before the next order. Gradually, I became aware of a rolling movement of the submarine's deck, like the movement of a rowboat with too much weight on one side, accompanied by the tilting of the periscopes sticking out of the sail. As we continued with the exercise, the rolling increased by larger and larger increments and some of the men had to grab the restraining cable at the deck's edge for balance. When the deck began to show a prominent sloping with each roll, the chief finally thanked us and ordered, "Secure from 'sally ship' exercise."

Remarkably, nobody said much of anything as the crew nonchalantly dispersed from the bizarre activity and returned to their various tasks. It wasn't clear to me how one should even ask Paul about the meaning of the event–"Did the sally go well, Chief?" Pushing aside my typical feeling of nearly total ignorance, I wandered toward him.

"It relates to the center of buoyancy, Dunham," Paul told me even before I asked. "The rolling provides data for calculating the metacentric height, important for determining the stability of the *Viperfish*–if we roll far enough to both sides, sufficient data are generated and the design engineers are happy. After our shipyard overhaul, several of the weights inside the boat have shifted to new positions, changing the center of buoyancy. When we surface out there," he pointed in the direction of the Pacific Ocean, "these factors can affect our stability. If the weight distribution is wrong, if the center of buoyancy has shifted too far down, it is possible for the first wave that hits us to roll us completely over. This kind of thing would lead to considerable crew discomfort and a probable immediate sinking."

I stared at the man, my mind trying to comprehend such a disaster. *Considerable* crew discomfort if the *Viperfish* rolled over?

He smiled brightly. "Therefore, it's the kind of thing we like to check out."

I returned to my qualifications work with a new worry. It would enter my mind every time we surfaced, as I waited to see if that first wave to slam against the side of the submarine would cause considerable crew discomfort.

The next day, the pier alongside the *Viperfish* was filled with activity. We loaded an endless supply of spare parts, crates of food, fuel oil for our diesel engine, and everything else each man on the boat could think of to sustain his existence at sea. The whole process reminded me of the packing adventures my family used to have before a camping trip. Rushing back and forth around the house, my mother gathered whatever she thought we might need for our trip to the forest or the beach. On a camping trip, however, we could count on certain basic elements essential to existence–oxygen, fresh air, maps, gas stations, warmth, and plenty of room to roam about.

On board the submerged *Viperfish*, we would be working to survive in an environment hostile to human life. We had to make our own air by producing oxygen and "scrubbing" (removing) away the carbon dioxide and carbon monoxide. To cool the excessive reactor-generated heat, we needed powerful air-conditioning systems; on the other hand, we had to provide warmth to the forward areas of the boat that became chilled from the cold waters around us. We had to navigate under the ocean where there were no stars or sky, create fresh water from the brine of the sea, and carefully monitor our uranium fuel reserves because no reactor refueling services were available on the high seas. For those of the crew who enjoyed hiking about, nothing could be done to accommodate them in the constrained spaces and cramped quarters. There was almost no room to roam–that was a daily fact of submarine life.

I had just finished storing a pocketbook, a box of cigars, and four fresh oranges inside the bunk locker beneath my rack when Marc Birken walked up to the crew's berthing area.

"Aloha, bruddah," he said to me, grinning widely and relishing his newly acquired Hawaiian dialect. "What's happening?"

I pointed to the oranges. "Fresh fruit for the long trip, in case we run out."

He looked at my oranges. "We're only going to be gone for a week or two," he said.

"Or three, or four–"

"Two weeks, or even three weeks, that's nothing! Wait until we go out for two months or even longer. Did I ever tell you about the time I dropped a garbage weight when the *Boone* was on one of our two-month Polaris patrols?"

I closed my bunk locker and pulled the curtain across the opening of my tiny home. "What's a garbage weight?" I asked.

His eyes lit up and his face became animated as he savored the memory of his story. "It was terrible! The thing made a hell of a noise! We were on station and rigged for quiet operations, no noise tolerated. When I saw the damn thing falling toward the deck, I tried to catch it. I tried to kick my shoe under it to break the fall. I tried everything I could, but it just slammed onto the steel plate like a damn sledge hammer that probably reverberated sound energy for thousands of miles across the ocean. I just about freaked out–it made a noise that almost blew the earphones off our sonarmen."

"Marc, what's a garbage weight?"

"And so," he clapped his hands together in front of me, "bam! The result was just like that! The instant the thing hit the metal, the captain was out of his stateroom, down the passageway, down the ladder, into the galley, and into my face."

"Holy Christ, the captain came to the galley? What did you tell him?"

"I told him I wanted to shoot myself. I told him the damn garbage weight weighed five tons, and it slipped from my hand. I told him I was sorry."

"Did he court-martial you?"

Marc grinned again. "It would have been better if he had, or if he had just beat the hell out of me because, God knows, I deserved it. But he decided to conduct a special training session in the forward torpedo room."

"What did he train you to do?"

"He trained me to move garbage weights from the starboard side of the ship to the port side. Then he trained me to move them back to the starboard side without dropping them. And then back to the port side, and then the starboard side. For *two hours*, he sat there staring at me with death in his eyes as I moved hundreds of garbage weights back and forth across the boat."

Marc then took me to the galley and showed me the small but incredibly heavy cast-iron weights used to sink the garbage ejected from the submarine. They came in tiny boxes, all stacked in cupboards near the garbage disposal unit. Each box of these devices weighed about twenty-five pounds.

That afternoon, Marc and I were assigned to join with the crew and load a couple thousand more weights. It took about fifty men to complete the job, a miserable and sweating process in the tropical sun. We transferred the boxes from a truck alongside the pier and handed them, one at a time, across the brow (gangway), over the deck, through the control-room hatch, down the ladder, into the galley, and finally into the storage locker. When we finished the task, I was sure that our center of buoyancy had shifted another ten feet. I began to worry again about our rolling over when that first wave nailed us after surfacing.

That evening was the last time available for liberty before going to sea. I planned to write a quick letter to my parents before joining Marc for a final steaming session in Waikiki. By then, I had everything necessary for the voyage packed into the tiny spaces available for personal items, and I was ready to go to sea. My fresh dungaree clothing had been stashed around the oranges and books in my bunk locker, and I was ahead of schedule with my qualifications work. A few liberty hours would clear my head for the submerged voyage.

I had just finished the last page of my letter and was preparing to depart to the barracks for the usual quick shower and a change to civvies when Bruce Rossi caught me.

"Dunham," he said, his voice characteristically tough, "I want you to help Petty Officer Nicholson with the reactor start-up tomorrow morning."

He didn't wait for an answer as he turned away and stomped in the direction of the engine room. I had already learned that a "start-up of the reactor" was considerably different from something like turning a key, which energizes most other kinds of engines. The process did not occur quickly nor could it be done casually. A reactor start–up was intense. It required long hours of painstaking checking and double–checking the calibration and accuracy of virtually every single electronic instrument in the engine room. The reactor could be started by one man, but, considering the complexity, it was easier done by two, even if one of the men was a trainee like me. Every single word on page after page of instructions in the start–up manual had to be followed, with religious–like adherence, in order to satisfy the general policy of "verbatim compliance."

If one deviated by so much as a word from the written instructions, the baggy pants of Rear Adm. Hyman G. Rickover, the Navy's director of nuclear propulsion, would appear on the horizon as another naval career crashed and burned.

The process was scheduled to begin in the engine room at midnight. A cold brew at Fort DeRussy was out of the question, as was a late–night *Viperfish* tour with adventuresome ladies. On start–up night, there would be no steaming, no drinking, no nocturnal adventures, no nothing but intense preparation while the rest of the crew slept. I had already come to know the mustached smiling face of Randy Nicholson, one of the three qualified reactor operators who had helped me with qualifications. At midnight, I strolled into the engine room and greeted Petty Officer Nicholson. We began the process to start up the reactor and worked through the night.

At exactly 0800 the next morning, the captain ordered the first backing bell (a pointer device in the engine room that showed the desired throttle speed) to move us away from Pearl Harbor's submarine pier. Again, Jim McGinn and I were sitting side by side in the engine room in front of the steam plant control panel's large rubber–coated throttle wheels to control steam to the propulsion turbines. We felt, as much as heard, the grinding sound of another camel being thrashed outside our pressure hull. Because the requirements of the steam plant control panel job were limited to opening or closing the propulsion turbine throttles on command, there was little we could do wrong. Nearby, the electrical operator and reactor operator sat in front of their panels to observe closely everything relating to electrical power and nuclear power, respectively. The engineering officer paced back and forth behind them, his eyes roaming across their panels, watching each meter, studying fluctuations in voltage and neutron levels, with the intent of keeping all of the vital systems in the engine room operating properly. The *Viperfish* was going to sea, and everybody was doing their jobs to ensure that nothing went wrong.

About five minutes later, with no warning, the captain suddenly hollered "Back emergency! Back emergency!" over the loudspeaker, his normally soft voice replaced by an urgent call for action. Instantly behind us, Bruce Rossi was watching us and monitoring every move as Jim and I bolted to our feet and struggled to crank the "ahead" throttles shut before turning the smaller wheel that reversed the direction of the screws. To make matters more difficult, a loud "reverse direction" alarm built into the steam control system began blaring a warning about throttle conflicts as Rossi bellowed, "Hurry, hurry, hurry!"

Jim and I were both sweating and hyperventilating by the time the turbines began their characteristic high–pitched screams in the reverse (backing) direction. We struggled to stop the *Viperfish* and back her away from whatever freighter or other threat was before us.

I loudly announced to the engineering officer that we were now answering the back–emergency bell at the same moment that the captain's voice, more relaxed this time, came over the loudspeakers: "All stop. All ahead one third."

From the sound of the captain's voice, it was apparent that the imminent danger had passed. Jim and I lightened our tight grip on our throttle wheels as we took our seats and answered the new bell. Both of us were sure that our quick reactions had saved the boat.

Marc strolled down the passageway at about that time. His grin was bigger than usual. "I was just up in the control center," he said. "Nice job you guys did answering that bell so fast."

"Thanks, Marc," I said, appreciating his recognition of our prompt reaction. "Did you get a look at what we almost hit?"

His smile faded. "Almost hit? We almost hit something?"

"Isn't that what the back–emergency bell was for?" I asked, starting to feel uncomfortable.

"That is what it *can* be for, but the captain just wanted to demonstrate to one of the junior officers on the bridge how quickly the *Viperfish* can stop. The training of the newer officers is one of his top priorities, and probably one of his greatest challenges. Unfortunately, this boat has a weird envelope of performance, and training is a formidable task."

"Oh. So it was a drill kind of a thing. Did we stop fast?"

"You guys answered the bell fast, and we started churning the water real nice, but it took us damn near forever to slow down. This thing don't wanna stop, no matter how fast you answer bells."

"We're too big," I speculated, thinking about the appearance of the *Viperfish* in dry dock.

"We are much too big for a decent submarine," he mumbled and wandered off to other tasks.

Feeling dumb, Jim and I clutched the throttles as we waited for the next "emergency."

Obviously, it would be difficult for us to figure out what was going on elsewhere in the submarine. Inside the engine–room hull, where there were no windows and no information about depth or speed, it was easy to visualize the worst possible disaster at the slightest provocation: The back–emergency bell became a terrible impending collision; the blast of an alarm from the steam panel, a major steam leak; the alarm horns over the reactor panel, an unsafe nuclear reactor condition or something even worse. This phenomenon, we were to discover, was especially a problem during intense activities when several alarms were shrieking, men were shouting, and turbines were screaming. This was the curse of working in the engine room. We spent an inordinate amount of time wondering just exactly what was happening elsewhere in the boat.

The *Viperfish* finally reached the ocean, as evidenced by the pitching and rolling of her hull. Cruising on the surface, she had moved several miles away from Oahu when a voice on the loud-speaker tersely announced the dive.

"Dive, dive!" were the only words called out by the chief of the watch at the ballast control panel. We heard no Klaxon noises or other horns, and there was nothing to suggest that this dive, the first since the *Viperfish*'s refit, was anything other than a routine event. It was the first submarine dive of my life, however, and I had already identified thousands of mechanical components that could potentially sink us if they failed while we were submerged. Everything about the dive was significant to me.

Idle conversation throughout the *Viperfish* immediately came to a halt. The men, intensifying their concentration on the systems in front of them, watched for anything that could increase the dangers to 120 men moving beneath the sea. Outside the pressure hull, large valves trapping the ballast air that gave us positive buoyancy suddenly flew open, quickly venting the outside tanks. The tanks began to fill with water, which caused the boat to develop negative buoyancy and become heavier. The massive bulk of the *Viperfish* rapidly settled down into the water, the bow angling downward as the two planesmen, who sat side by side at the diving station, pressed forward on their wheels controlling the diving planes. All sensations of movement from wave activity came to a halt. Abruptly, we felt frozen in space as the bulk of the superstructure and sail dropped below the surface of the ocean.

Sandy Gallivan, chief of the watch at the ballast control panel, opened the ballast tank vent valves. He flipped switches to start and stop pumps in the bowels of the submarine, thus controlling the transfer of water and fine-tuning the boat's buoyancy and balance. In the engine room, Randy Nicholson adjusted the reactor controls to maintain adequate steam energy for the propulsion turbines. Donald Svedlow, sitting next to him, controlled the electrical systems. Diving required tightly coordinated choreography of machinery and highly trained men. From one end of the boat

to the other, the men were working, watching, thinking, and continuously seeking optimal performance from the equipment
under their control.

The captain scanned the ocean surface through the starboard
periscope. He ordered the diving officer to have the planesmen
maintain periscope depth and zero angle, in order to leave nothing above the surface of the water but the small tubes and lenses
of the two periscopes.

"Now, attention all hands!" the captain called through the 1MC
loudspeakers, "The ship is at periscope depth. All hands check for
leaks!"

The captain was directing everyone on board–the enlisted men
and officers, the scientists in the bow compartment, and the few
civilian shipyard technicians along for the sea trials–to search for
any seawater leaks that could suddenly flood the boat and kill us
all. This extremely serious business precluded the joking and light
banter among crew members that usually occurred during their
routine tasks of running the boat. There was nothing routine
about searching for flaws in the dry dock modifications, during
which so many pressure boundaries had been opened and
welded shut again.

The entire process was simultaneously intense and inspiring.
There was a powerful awareness of being surrounded by the dark
pressures of our submerged existence. We could almost feel the
suffocating enclosure of the ocean as we committed ourselves to
the experience of moving below its surface.

With flashlights in hand, we peered into every dark recess;
studied each cluster of pipes filled with seawater; and scrutinized
every valve, pipe flange, and pressure hull fitting. We waved our
lights toward the oily waters of the bilge to look for rising levels
and studied the curved steel on the inside of the pressure hull as
we searched for tiny telltale streams of salt water. We listened
carefully for the hissing sounds of hidden high–pressure leaks that
could expand and rupture the hull when we moved deeper into
the ocean. The USS *Viperfish* was our declared sanctuary from the

outside forces of nature, and we would allow no violations of her integrity.

During the next five hours, we moved deeper into the ocean in 100-foot increments. At each level of our descent, we searched for leaks. As the pressure around us increased, a parallel force in our minds began to develop, a psychological pressure further riveting our attention on the job before us.

When the captain called over the loudspeaker, "Rig ship for deep submergence," we were ready to take the final step of easing our boat into the deepest and darkest corner of our submergence envelope, where the extreme pressures of the Pacific Ocean could further threaten our world inside the *Viperfish.*

The doors between the compartments were now locked and dogged tightly shut, isolating the crew into small pockets of men throughout the submarine.* I moved slowly up and down the engine room passageways as I examined the clusters of seawater pipes around me and checked for anything that looked abnormal. If flooding occurred from a broken pipe–a sudden disaster of roaring high-pressure water at that depth–none of us in the engine room would survive. Instant death would be certain. All of us had known of this risk when we volunteered for submarine duty. The remainder of the crew might have a chance of survival *if* the boat was able to surface quickly enough, *if* the reactor stayed operational long enough, and *if* the design of the *Viperfish* allowed for sufficient buoyancy.

Another dark fact from my qualifications work emerged. Should flooding occur in the huge Special Project compartment and high-pressure seawater flooded the cavernous hangar space in the front third of the ship, the weight of the water would certainly take all of us straight to the bottom. The Soviet Navy had

---

* To maintain the watertight integrity of the compartments, each massive steel door between compartments has a central handle and a series of clamps that seal the door when the handle is turned. A door is "dogged" when the handle is turned, thus sealing the door.

already lost a submarine in this manner, years before, when the hangar space in a Whisky twin–cylinder missile submarine flooded. To make a bad situation worse, the Special Project hangar compartment was the one space in the *Viperfish* with a huge hole penetrating the bottom of the hull.

I directed my flashlight toward the clusters of pipes carrying seawater to the propulsion systems and wondered how long the reactor could provide useful power if one of the pipes ruptured and the engine room was lost. The loss of the USS *Thresher* was in the background of our consciousness, always suppressed, yet always present. The details of her sinking in 1963 had never been fully clarified by the Navy Department. Presumably, she was lost, with 129 men on board, because of an engine–room leak, and her engineering problems were quickly compounded by the SCRAM* of her reactor and ice clogging in the high–pressure blowing system, which prevented her from surfacing. That was the year I had joined the Navy. Hopefully, after three years, the engineers responsible for the design parameters of U.S. submarines had modified the *Viperfish* under the safety provisions of the SUBSAFE program (a comprehensive retrofit program developed to prevent another such disaster).

We finally reached our test depth, the deepest allowed for the *Viperfish*, and we studied our seawater pipes. We would never intentionally move below this depth. The performance envelope of the *Viperfish* was not designed for deeper penetration or greater pressures. There was only one defined level below that point–the depth associated with the end of a submarine's life, the crush depth, from which nobody returns. When a submarine moves

---

* SCRAM refers to "safety control reactor ax man," a term given to the man responsible for cutting the rope holding the control rods out of an experimental reactor core during a test at the University of Chicago. When the rods dropped back into the core, the reactor was shut down. Although the system for shutting down a nuclear reactor is now profoundly different, the term SCRAM, meaning a total and complete emergency shutdown, has been retained.

through this final pressure limit, sonar systems for hundreds of miles around pick up the strange sounds of bursting pipes and collapsing bulkheads, the curious staccato of the dying submarine's screams, like the rapid popping of popcorn, as the vessel implodes upon herself and plunges to the ocean floor.

Captain Gillon finally announced that the *Viperfish* was free of leaks at our test depth. We planed up, blew the water out of our ballast tanks, and thundered up to the surface, where 120 men began to breathe easily again.

DRILLS AND MORE DRILLS

THROUGHOUT THE SECOND HALF of 1966, the Vietnam conflict continued to escalate, and record numbers of aircraft missions were flown against enemy targets north of the Demilitarized Zone (DMZ). The Soviet Communist Party newspaper *Pravda* criticized President Lyndon B. Johnson's peace overtures and blasted the United States for its armed interference in the internal affairs of foreign countries. The Soviet Defense Ministry newspaper *Krasnaya Zvezda* reported that increasing numbers of Russian military experts were training North Vietnamese antiaircraft missile crews to improve the fire-power of their weapons against the Americans. At the same time, Soviet Deputy Premier Vladimir Novikov pledged increased eco-nomic and military assistance to Hanoi.

On 6 September 1966, Pfc James A. Johnson, Jr., received a dis-honorable discharge and was sentenced to five years at hard labor for refusing to go to Vietnam; on 29 September, the U.S. Military Assistance Command in Saigon reported United States combat fatalities in Vietnam had reached 5,302. The Institute of Strategic Studies reported in London that the Soviet Union had surrounded

Moscow and Leningrad with antiballistic missile defenses, while increasing its number of medium bombers to 1,200 (compared with the U.S. total of 222). At the same time, the institute reported, Communist China was developing a ballistic missile delivery system for nuclear weapons.

Meanwhile, Soviet submarines from Vladivostok patrolled their assigned sectors in the Pacific Ocean. Some of them sought contact with ships from other countries, but others, lying silently in wait, constituted a submerged threat for the launching of ballistic and cruise missiles at targets in the United States. The sounds of cavitation (loud noises of collapsing air bubbles spinning off high-speed screws) carried into the water around the nuclear and conventional submarines as they left port and pushed their propulsion systems to 100 percent power. Upon reaching their maximum speeds in the Sea of Japan, their characteristic acoustic signatures moved through the high–pressure waters that dropped three miles below each vessel and finally reached the listening microphones of the U.S. SOSUS array. Thousands of miles away, DIA (Defense Intelligence Agency) communications specialists patiently listened to the sounds of moving Soviet submarines as vector equipment identified coordinates that could provide potentially useful information for the United States.

▼

Life on a submarine stretches the boundaries of human behavior. Psychologists have long studied the reactions of people to the presence of surrounding humanity in the cities of our society. They define an individual's "private zone" as a few feet of space around that person; regular encroachment on the private zone by others can annoy the individual and perhaps result in irrational behavior. Such violations of privacy can be tolerated for short intervals, such as within a crowded bus or an elevator, but when the time is extended beyond an hour or two, behavior and performance can suffer accordingly. Encroachment on individuals' private zones often is used as an explanation for hostile and antisocial acts within crowded apartment buildings of our inner cities. The only practical solution might be to escape frequently to open spaces where the mind can regain a normal perspective, but this is usually impossible.

To understand the feeling of living enclosed within the *Viperfish,* one can visualize 120 men confined to a small house with four big rooms, several smaller rooms, and no telephone or television. The windows are blackened and sealed shut, the doors are bolted with multiple padlocks, and no communication is allowed with anyone outside the house. No women are allowed within the house, and there are only memories of the pleasures from prior relationships. The men have no way to determine if it is day or night outside, and it quickly becomes apparent that the time of day really does not matter. Everyone inside the house is aware that forces of nature can suddenly destroy the house without warning and that forces generated by other clusters of men living within the neighborhood can also result in abrupt destruction.

Movies are shown and good meals are served, but the men know that no doors or windows to the outside world will be opened for a period lasting up to two months. The house has a mission, the men are told, but the nature of the mission is never revealed to any but those who have been appointed to head the household. The performance of tasks within this house is done not just because of the military imperative, but because every single man confined within believes in the mission, whatever it might be. From the driving force of this belief comes the possibility of success and the probability of survival during the long days of confinement. In our case, the house was called the USS *Viperfish.*

In the middle of the first night on board the boat, as we were steaming at a depth of about three hundred feet, I learned about "blowing the head."

It is not easy to flush anything into the outside ocean from a deeply submerged vessel. Because the external water pressure at three hundred feet is in the range of 150 pounds per square inch, a pressure greater than this must be generated to propel waste products out of the submarine. Even the most efficient toilet can produce no more than a few ounces of pressure to expel waste. Any flushing attempt would result in a geyser of high-pressure seawater blasting into the head, immediately flooding the entire compartment, and potentially sinking the submarine.

The *Viperfish* head, therefore, was designed with a septic tank (called the sanitary tank) of great strength. Located directly under the rows of toilets and showers, the tank acted as a storage place for waste products until it was convenient to empty it. Because the tank was normally maintained at atmospheric pressure, the commodes (toilets), showers, and sinks could easily empty into the device.

None of these technical considerations was in my mind when I awakened in the middle of my first night at sea with a compelling need to use the facility. Dim lights, always on in the head (sailors' term for bathroom), day and night, illuminated the solid steel interior. Everything was made of steel—the deck (floor), the showers, the mirrors, and the commode, including its ice-cold seat. The head was generally a spooky place, always too dark, and always smelling bad no matter how vigorously the men worked to keep it clean.

Dressed only in my skivvies (undershorts—nobody wore pajamas to bed), I swung out of my rack and hiked barefoot down the dim red-lit corridors to the head. The cold steel of the deck and commode seat jolted me awake.

After using the commode, I began the sequence of valve operations to flush it. Opening the first valve allowed one to see the sloshing fluids in the dark recesses in the tank. I immediately discovered that it was necessary to avoid breathing the concentrated odors of methane, hydrogen, and other explosive gases bubbling forth from below. I then turned the other valves behind the commode in exactly the correct sequence as I had been taught, and seawater finally flushed through the bowl for a thorough washing-out operation.

Before I had time to reflect on my success at flushing, Larry Kanen entered the room with a rush and began scurrying around, sealing drain valves in the sinks, showers, and decking.

"What are you doing, Larry?" I asked.

"Gonna blow the head, Roger!" he announced with remarkable enthusiasm.

I had no idea what he was talking about, but it was obvious that he was intent on completing his job as quickly as possible.

"Do I have time to rinse my hands?"

"Better hurry! Gotta blow the head, right away!"

Kanen finished his work, sealing every valve in the head. A few seconds later, a hissing, gurgling sound began to emerge from the drains as he turned a compressed-air valve to blow high-pressure air into the sanitary tank, some of which leaked up from around the valves and back into the head. As the pressure in the tank increased, the contents of the tank blasted out into the ocean.

The odor filling the head from the bubbling drains was intense. Fighting back a gagging feeling, I returned to my rack and yanked the curtain across the opening. When I took a couple of deep breaths, I discovered that the escape was short-lived. Fifty feet in front of my rack was a vent line designed to relieve the pressure remaining in the tank after the flushing. For the next fifteen minutes, as Kanen vented the tank, the hissing gas that smelled like a nightmare concoction of rotting eggs filled our sleeping area. It penetrated the entire compartment—our bunks, our hair, our nostrils, and everything we owned.

We spent two more weeks in the waters west of Oahu to practice diving down to the level of our test depth and climbing back to the surface again. With radical movements of the rudder and control planes, the captain performed various "angles and dangles" that placed the *Viperfish* every conceivable position that a submarine could manage. We tested each piece of equipment for any flawed circuits or machinery that could endanger our lives or limit the success of our mission. The sonarmen adjusted their controls as they listened to the strange sounds of whales moving through the ocean, the torpedomen and fire control technicians calibrated their equipment, and the nukes shut down and started up their turbogenerators and the nuclear reactor. The newer men on the ship became better acquainted with the veterans, and we all learned the essentials of living, training, and working together in the claustrophobic quarters of the *Viperfish*.

In the hangar compartment, the Special Project engineers, strolling around, looked down from time to time into the huge hole that penetrated the decking. Commander Spiegel and Lieutenant Dobkin worked with the civilians and photographer Robbie Teague to ensure that the Fish equipment worked properly. They weren't hostile to the rest of us; they were just private. If one of the regular crew came by, they lowered their voices. They nodded to the crewman and said, "Hi." The crewman nodded back and said, "Hi," and that was the end of the conversation. If any of us lingered, a heavy silence descended over the hangar until the outsider left the immediate area.

On one occasion, while I was struggling to learn a particularly difficult system in the hangar, I asked Lieutenant Dobkin a question relating to their work. The question was apparently too sensitive because his response amounted to a lecture on the nature of the "silent service."

"Submarines are the silent service because we remain silent about these kinds of things," he said, his eyes staring straight at me before finally turning away to join his civilian associates. I felt a flash of anger and mentally debated why our Special Project wasn't like any other part of our submarine–everything else we worked with was also a part of the silent service. I returned to my qualifications work with silent service philosophies moving through my mind. Finally resolving the problem, I decided that the Special Project was, simply enough, top secret and therefore different from everything else we did that was just secret. Years later, I would discover that the Special Project was, in fact, *compartmentalized* top secret; not even an individual with a top secret clearance could learn the details of our mission.

Six days before we returned to Pearl Harbor, the word spread through the boat that we would be starting torpedo-firing exercises. This was exactly what I had been waiting for since the day I volunteered for submarine duty. Shooting torpedoes was a fundamental operation of submarines, an essence of sorts. It provided for the boat's survival and established her effectiveness as a military machine. After several hours had passed with no further information about the exercise, I climbed into my rack and began fading off to sleep.

The captain's voice suddenly blared over the loudspeaker system: "Now, man battle stations torpedo! Man battle stations torpedo!"

I popped my eyes open, leaped to the deck, and ran at top speed down the narrow passageway in the direction of the engine room. At the same time, the other men jumped out of their racks and raced toward their battle stations. Everybody dodged each other in a state of high-speed, controlled movement to reach their assigned positions in the *Viperfish*. I ducked under the sharp-edged valves in the tunnel over the reactor and climbed through the watertight door opening to the engine room and my battle station: the turbine throttle wheels that Jim and I had controlled when we left Pearl Harbor. Jim was nowhere to be seen, and so I placed my hands on both wheels and waited for the excitement to begin.

In the control center, two hundred feet in front of the throttles, the captain looked through the periscope, spotted the torpedo recovery ship that had arrived from Pearl Harbor to help us, and ordered the exercise to begin. Several junior officers, working on their torpedo qualifications, moved through the established routine and prepared to fire our torpedoes from the hangar compartment in the bow.

While they performed their work, I sat stiffly upright in front of the large rubberized engine-room throttles and wondered when something would happen. Surrounded by the other men in the engine room, all of whom were also waiting for something to happen, I was unaware of the frenzied activity in the control center as the torpedo fire control technicians, torpedomen, and officers tracked and plotted the shoot. Half an hour later, I turned to ask the engineering officer when we were going to fire the first torpedo. At that instant, I felt a slight shudder of the *Viperfish's* hull and heard the distant "whooshing" of a missile being launched into the ocean.

That was all there was to the shot. I stood up, gripped the throttle wheels, and waited expectantly for the control center to order sudden changes in our speed. Remarkably, the bell indicator remained silent, and there were no further orders. None of us did anything except stare at our control panels as the captain announced over the speaker system, "Now, surface, surface, surface."

With the usual amount of gurgling sounds, we broke the surface. After the first of an endless number of huge waves hit the side of the *Viperfish,* we began aimlessly wandering around searching for the torpedo we had just fired. It was designed to run a specific distance before running out of fuel and floating to the surface, where it could be recovered and fired again—a sort of Navy recycling system. The torpedo was also programmed to release a brilliant yellow dye to make it easier to spot. The captain and officers who had fired the shot searched through their binoculars from their vantage point at the top of the sail, sixty-five feet above the water. The two lookouts in the back of the cockpit scanned the whitecaps in the opposite direction with their binoculars. Somewhere near the horizon, the crew of the heaving torpedo recovery ship also scanned the ocean for any trace of the torpedo.

In the maneuvering area of the engine room, we began to feel like we were dying. I knew there was going to be a major problem, after the first twenty minutes on the surface, when I sensed the beginning stages of a sickening pain in the center of my abdomen. I looked down at the black coffee splashing over the top of my cup and felt a surge of nausea, immediately followed by a sweating attack of vertigo. Our rounded hull, designed for submerged operations, did little to diminish the effects of the powerful waves. Each time we rolled thirty degrees to the left or right, we instantly came up and rolled almost as far in the other direction.

The waves continued to batter against us with increasing force. As we rolled violently back and forth, pungent oil fumes from the bilge water permeated the hot and humid air around us. My throat constricted from the gagging odor of the fumes and my eyes blurred, but I tightened my sweaty fists around the throttle wheels.

Randy Nicholson, his face pale and showing stress, sat behind me and watched the reactor control panel pitching up and down in front of him. Next to him was the powerful frame of Donald Svedlow, a longtime veteran of the Submarine Service, who also looked like he wanted to be anywhere but on the surface of the ocean. Our sweating engineering officer, Lt. (jg) Douglas Katz, paced a fixed pattern in the corner of the maneuvering area. His skin was a sickly green color, and his tortured eyes repeatedly gazed across the engine room as though he were searching for the horizon.

My dungaree shirt turned a dark blue from sweat as I fought the nausea. I began repeatedly swallowing and belching, and there was a ringing sound in my ears. I prayed for them to find the torpedo, and then I prayed for them to forget the torpedo. Finally, I cursed all torpedoes as I visualized helicopters flying in to lift me off the boat.

Glancing at the men around me, I wondered who was going to lose it first. The sloshing of coffee from my cup onto the decking created curious miniature rivers moving in opposite directions in response to the roll of the boat. I began to eye the tall metal trash can clamped next to the throttle wheels, and I wondered how I could quickly utilize it without attracting everybody's attention. It seemed reasonable that throwing up should be a private thing, but there was no way to leave my battle station to seek the relative isolation of the head. I thought about the civilians in the hangar compartment and grimaced at the thought of their breakfasts being lost into the huge hole in the center of their Special Project area.

Forty-five minutes into the search for the wayward torpedo, Lieutenant Katz cleared his throat a couple of times and left the area. He mumbled something about checking out the vacuum in one of our condensers.

"He's gonna puke," Svedlow grumbled after Katz's staggering form was out of sight. "He's gonna put his head into the bilge and he's gonna search for Ralph O'Roark."

"We're *all* gonna puke, bruddah," Nicholson said, wiping the sweat from his forehead. "It's just a matter of time."

"Goddamn forward pukes and their goddamn forward puke torpedoes," Svedlow growled, followed by the longest belching sound I had ever heard.

"The forward pukes are gonna make us puke," Nicholson said, grimly. "I'll pay for the goddamn torpedo myself. Just dive this thing and send me the bill."

Incredibly, Svedlow then pulled out a pack of cigars from his shirt pocket and asked if anybody wanted a smoke. Nicholson grabbed one, and soon the entire maneuvering area of the engine room carried a layer of pale cigar smoke mixing with the odors of diesel oil fumes and sweat. The psychology of cigar smoke at a time of end-stage nausea was not clear to me, but it appeared to be a well-established practice.

My mouth became dry, and a terrible taste began to emerge from the back of my throat. I turned to Svedlow, "Got an extra cigar?" I asked.

As the smoke became thicker, we all heard the upper engine-room watch shouting in the direction of our starboard condenser. I looked down the passageway, where the watchstander, a burly machinist mate with an evil grin on his face, was leaning over the hole in the deck leading to the bilge below.

"He ain't down there, sir!" he hollered at the top of his lungs.

The machinist mate waited a moment and his grin became bigger. "Ralph O'Roark ain't down there, Mr. Katz!"

The distant voice of an anguished engineering officer, floating into the thick air around us, shouted something appropriately obscene to the machinist mate. The prolonged vomiting sounds of "O'Roark!" then carried up to us, as a group of men from various corners of the upper–level engine room quickly gathered around the hole.

"He ain't down there, sir!" they shouted in unison.

We continued searching for the lost torpedo for another fifteen minutes as hundreds of waves battered the hull. Puffing my cigar furiously, I tried to concentrate on peaceful green pastures, a walk in the woods, clouds in the sky, anything besides throwing up.

It was hopeless.

Like a malignant epidemic spreading through the boat, the condition of terminal vomiting finally struck everyone in the maneuvering area, including myself. By the time the captain gave up on finding the torpedo and we dove into the quiet waters below, almost the entire crew had been informed that Ralph O'Roark, the venerable ghost of American submarine bilges, was not and would never be "down there."

We steamed up the Pearl Harbor channel a few days later, after confirming that the *Viperfish* was operational. My qualifications, progressing rapidly, were almost to the halfway mark. The maze of propulsion systems in the engine room became easier to learn when the equipment was in one piece. The captain was satisfied, the Fish was ready for future testing, and the *Viperfish* didn't have any leaks.

As soon as Marc Birken, working with the other electricians, had pulled the huge shore power cables from the pier to the *Viperfish*, we both raced up to the barracks, showered, and changed into civvies for a night in Waikiki. Even though we had been at sea for less than three weeks, it was a strange feeling to be suddenly exposed to the open spaces of Honolulu with its kaleidoscope of lights and human activity. Marc and I slowly cruised up and down Kalakaua Avenue in his TR–3, and I felt the impact of the scanty swimsuits worn by the hordes of beautiful women.

Even more amazing to me was the mental effect of seeing such ravishing femininity after weeks of confinement. It was a shocking kind of transition, going from the orderly life on the submarine to the females and music in the nightclubs of Honolulu.

We made our usual bar stop at Fort DeRussy before walking to the Waikiki strip. Soon, we were making moves on the dance floor at a popular nightclub near the Ilikai Hotel. The first woman I danced with was an attractive blonde who casually whispered in my ear that she was a "WestPac widow."

"I'm sorry to hear that," I told her sympathetically. The newspapers were filled with stories of men dying in Vietnam, many of them in the Navy and attached to the Western Pacific (WestPac) forces, and she was obviously trying to adjust to her loss. We danced for a few more minutes before I asked her if she was getting along okay.

"Getting along okay?" She backed away and looked at me.

"After the loss of your husband," I said, beginning to have an uncomfortable feeling.

Her voice lost its soft tone. "I'm a WestPac widow. You don't know what that means? My husband's on patrol off Vietnam for the next five or six months."

I stared at her as the meaning sank in. Although the music was still playing, I escorted her back to her seat without a word.

She looked up at me, angry now, her voice becoming harsh. "I wasn't enjoying the dance anyway," she said. "Besides, you smell like diesel oil."

Fuming, I returned to my seat and looked at the expensive pineapple shell filled with watered-down rum in front of me. I grabbed the drink and sipped the miserable mixture until our waitress stopped by and placed change on the receipt tray from the forty dollars I had handed her. Before I had a chance to reach for the tray, her long blond hair passed in front of my face and the money was suddenly gone.

Marc caught up with me as I stormed out of the nightclub. "Hey, bruddah, you okay?" he asked.

"I'm okay! I'm just fine! One gal's playing around on her husband. Another steals our money. These people don't care that we're working our tails off for our country."

"Wait a minute," Marc said. "Those are probably just a couple of losers. I'm sure we can–"

"Besides, the gal I was dancing with told me that I smelled like diesel oil."

He looked at me and smiled. "She said that? Really?"

"Really."

"Well, my girl was much more polite. She told me that I had a 'curious' smell. A mixture of something strange with something else strange. I noticed she didn't want to dance too close, either"

"We showered," I said. "We *tried* to get clean."

"We can't smell that bad. I used plenty of soap and after–shave lotion."

We both agreed that there was little promise for a midnight tour of the *Viperfish* and that the entire evening had been about as much fun as blowing the sanitary tanks. Declaring a major defeat for the military, we drove back to the Enlisted Men's Club of Pearl Harbor. We found a couple of comfortable chairs, listened to some superb music, and became obliterated in the company of Old Granddad until the early morning hours.

The next day, Captain Gillon announced that a swimming pool would be built on the topside deck of the *Viperfish*. After we stopped laughing, he explained the problems of rotating a gigantic submarine when she is barely moving through the water. Throughout our sea trials, it had been apparent that the submerged *Viperfish* was unable to turn efficiently in a small space at slow speed. Handling like an airplane, with the responsiveness of her control systems dependent on speed, she was sluggish and lethargic when she slowed to less than three knots. To resolve this problem, the shipyard workers built a hump on top of the original hump. The double-humped submarine looked even more bizarre than the original. The lower hump was part of the primary bat–cave structure; the new hump was simply a bow thruster, or water diverter, that had been designed to squirt jets of seawater out of either side of the hump. This gave the *Viperfish* a jet assist, so to speak, to improve her turns at slow speed. To force the water through the openings, a huge motor, which looked like a fat cannon, was welded to the front of the hump and aimed straight ahead.

Because the motor was so large, the wires connected to it were enormous. The electricians became excited about what kind of monster circuit breaker could be used to turn it on and off. Their stress levels increased when they thought about the huge motor's load on the electrical system, a load that might dim the lights and leave us without enough power for anything else. The captain therefore decided to test the thing before going to sea again by using shore power from gigantic cables stretching from the pier. Because the motor was in the air on the top deck and water was necessary for the test, we needed a pool.

The shipyard workers descended on the *Viperfish* again. Several hours later, a high circle of boards surrounded the bat–cave hump and the bow–thruster pump. The captain asked me to coordinate communications with the electricians after the pool was filled with Pearl Harbor water; I donned earphones and a microphone, and soon we were ready for the test.

"Are the electricians in the engine room ready?" the captain asked.

When I called down to the electricians, they were near the circuit breaker and ready to turn it on. "Yes, sir, ready to go!" I called out.

The captain inspected the pool a final time, and I noticed several crewmen from nearby submarines gathering at the edge of the pier to watch the test.

Finally, the captain was ready. Standing back from the area, he joined the Special Project engineers nearby and ordered, "Energize the thruster motor."

"Turn on the thruster motor!" I shouted into the microphone.

In the distant bowels of the ship, I heard a loud thumping

sound of the huge circuit breaker closing. The motor jumped as it came to life, blasting water out the sides of the diverter system. Water from the pool was sucked into the motor system as jets of water blew out the wooden sides of the pool. Several of the planks fell overboard, as others were swirled inside the pool and headed for the motor.

"Turn it off! Turn it off!" the captain hollered.

"Turn it off! Turn it off!" I called to the engine room. The motor ground to a halt just before one of the bigger planks was sucked into its blades.

I waited next to the demolished pool while the captain and engineers conferred about the test results and the near destruction of the motor. After considerable arm waving and debate, they finally decided that the energy consumption, the noise, and the motor's cumbersome inefficiency outweighed any potential benefit that might allow the *Viperfish* to make smaller turns. The electricians removed the cables, and the shipyard workers removed the planks and what was left of the swimming pool. For reasons never clear to me, they left the bow–thruster pump in place. For the next two years, we cruised around the ocean with a pump on a hump, both of them good for nothing.

We finally began loading supplies for the shakedown voyage across the Pacific Ocean to Seattle and San Francisco. Between loading more garbage weights and working on my seemingly endless qualifications, I took some time off to surf the then uncrowded waters at Ala Moana and spectacular Sunset Beach on the north shore. I used a long board and surfed as often as possible. The biggest problem was trying to protect my skin (now totally white as the result of three weeks spent under the ocean surface) from the bright tropical sunlight.

My evenings were free for steaming in Honolulu, and I took advantage of every minute. Thoughts of the upcoming submerged isolation fueled a compelling need for social adventures. Marc and I quickly recovered from our misfortunes in Waikiki. With vigorous scrubbing and the passage of a week or so, our residual submarine smell slowly faded and ladies once again enjoyed dancing with us.

Before leaving Oahu, we propelled the *Viperfish* across Pearl Harbor to a "deperming" station, where we spent a full day wrapping the boat's superstructure with electrical cables. It was nasty work in the hot Hawaiian sun, but morale was extremely high. Everybody worked enthusiastically to lower the thick wires into the water and pull them up on the other side of the boat until she was fully wrapped in wire.

After the final cable was pulled out of the water and bolted to the high–voltage generating station, we were all drenched in sweat and our hands were black from the rubber insulation around the cables. We were ordered to leave the immediate area so deperming could take place. This process used current generated by massive voltage to remove any magnetic fields in the *Viperfish* that could trigger the detonation of underwater mines. Because most of us still had no clue about our upcoming mission, any consideration of going into mine–infested waters was something that nobody wanted even to think about.

I packed more fruit into my bunk locker, stuffed in another box of cigars, and tucked some John D. MacDonald novels among my clothes. Most of us would wear the same dungarees or the new lint-free overalls called "faboomer suits" for a week at a time, so stocking fresh clothes was limited to one change per week. The trip to the mainland would take about a week. We each needed only three pairs of underclothing, dungaree shirts, and pants, in addition to dress blues, a black silk sailor tie, and a clean white sailor hat to wear during liberty in Seattle and San Francisco.

Just before we left Pearl Harbor, a new electrician, Brian Lane, reported on board the *Viperfish*. He was married and took a soft-spoken, low–key approach to the qualifications work that eventually would lead to his running the engine room's complex electrical control panel. As was the case for so many of us, this boat was Brian's first assignment after nuclear power training and submarine school. He quietly began studying the *Viperfish* systems under the watchful eye of Donald Svedlow and the other quali- fied electricians.

On a brilliantly sunny day, we steamed down the Pearl Harbor channel, rendered honors to the USS *Arizona* as we passed the general area of the sunken vessel, and departed Oahu. The crew shut and dogged the hatches on the topside deck, and the *Viperfish* moved out of the channel, past the Pearl Harbor ("Papa Hotel") demarcation point that marks the end of the channel, and into the deeper waters of the Pacific Ocean. With the announcement, "Dive! Dive!" the captain cleared the bridge; the lookouts raced down the ladder from the top of the sail and slammed the control room hatch shut as the chief of the watch hit the levers to open the ballast tank valves. Our white-foam wake lingered behind us like a long feathery trail that abruptly ended in a final swarm of bubbles as the ballast tanks filled with water and we angled down to a depth of three hundred feet below the surface. We pushed through the waters off Diamond Head on the east end of Oahu and aligned our navigation system for the Strait of Juan de Fuca at the U.S.–Canadian border–nine days and 2,500 miles away.

Feeling suspended in our submerged world hundreds of feet below the surface, which seemed much like floating to the far reaches of outer space, we were unaware of any movement to suggest that the *Viperfish* was, in fact, pushing her way through the ocean toward Seattle. In the engine room, we couldn't even tell if it was day or night because the bright white lights remained on continuously. All sense of direction and time became distorted as the days passed slowly and we had no sensory contact with the world around us.

For me, existence was a surrealistic process of waiting until the clock said it was quarter to twelve, at which time I assumed my watch at the steam throttles. It didn't matter if it was fifteen min- utes before noon or fifteen minutes before midnight, so long as I was sitting in front of the throttles at quarter to twelve. Twice each day, I repeated the process–climbing through the tunnel, walking down the upper-level engine-room passageway, and sitting down to begin my four-hour watch. Four hours later, I left the throttles for eight hours off watch. During this time, I wandered around and worked on qualifications or climbed into my rack and went to sleep.

If a movie was showing in the crew's dining area before I went on watch, I knew it was nighttime; otherwise, it was daytime. The crew's sleeping area was darkened twenty-four hours a day, so no matter when a crewman awakened it seemed like night. To resolve any lingering uncertainties between day and night, if I really wanted to know, I could climb up to the control center and see what lights were on. White lights indicated daytime and dim red lights meant that the sun had gone down and the world above us was dark. The red lights allowed the crew's pupils to dilate so that they could see better if the boat suddenly had to surface or move up to periscope depth. For the first few days, I tried to keep track of day and night, but I finally gave up because it was of no significance.

In the middle of the first week, I was tracking down some obscure system in the engine room when the sudden thunderous roar of flooding water drowned out the whining of the turbogenerators. I was in the upper-level area of the compartment at the time. Wedged between a heat exchanger and a bank of reactor control electronics, I was trying to read the number on a valve to identify its position on my schematic. I was tightly trapped between the solid steel of heavy equipment. For the next ten seconds, I fought furiously to free myself, while my mind screamed total terror and the loudspeakers announced the obvious.

"Now, flooding, flooding, flooding! We have flooding in the engine room! Lower level, starboard!" the engineering officer hollered. The lower-level engine room, similar to a basement, was below the main engine room and accessed by ladders connecting the two levels.

"Jesus Christ!" I hollered to nobody in particular as I finally popped free from the equipment and jumped into the central engine-room passageway. A herd of running machinist mates almost knocked me over, but I joined them in an all-out sprint down the passageway. As they disappeared down a ladder toward the bilge, I ran to the compartment's watertight door and began spinning the bar that dogged the door shut to isolate the engine room from the rest of the boat.

"Main seawater system, starboard condenser!" the engineering officer announced as the roaring noise became louder. "Lower-level engine room, isolate the starboard condenser!"

"Now, all hands, we have flooding in the engine room!" the captain's voice announced from the control center. "Surface, surface, surface!"

I began climbing down the ladder into the dark areas of the lower-level engine room. My hands shook violently as I tried to grip the ladder's steel sides. The roaring intensified as several other men and I moved closer into the area of the bilge; I knew there was little time before all the valves would be underwater and the engine room would be lost.

Suddenly, half the lights throughout the submarine went out, and I could hear the distant sound of high-voltage circuit breakers popping open. The lower-level engine room became darker, and the engineer announced, "Now, we have lost the starboard turbogenerator! Lower-level engine room, report the status of the flooding!"

The *Viperfish* assumed a steep up-angle. The screaming sound of the turbine propulsion system was deafening as we tried to accelerate toward the surface. I jumped off the ladder and landed on the steel plates above the bilge as the engine room lights flickered. Finally, I ran aft down the steeply angled decking toward the main condenser. The passageway was completely dry.

Looking around the area, I tried to find the source of the flooding. On the outboard side of the passageway, a pipe with an open valve was blasting water straight down into the bilge. Several men were sitting next to the condenser, all with big grins on their faces, and ignoring the roar. Milling around the passageway were the machinist mates who had jumped down the ladder in front of me; they were also grinning. One of them, more sympathetic than the rest, told me that the ballast control panel operator was pumping the water overboard as fast as it came out of the pipe.

Bruce Rossi handed me the communications headset as a chief machinist mate reached down and cranked the valve shut.

"Tell the engineer we have isolated the flooding, Dunham," Bruce said.

I stared at the men as I pressed down on the microphone button. "Maneuvering, this is the lower-level engine room," I barked into the communications microphone. "We have found the leak, and we have isolated the flooding."

"Very well," someone replied. Immediately, the captain's voice broadcast over the ship's main loudspeaker system: "Now, secure from flooding drill, secure from flooding drill."

And, so, that is how I learned about submarine drills.

The drills, always realistic to the extreme, forced us to react intentionally and automatically, improving our response time. The concept of "only a drill" allowed a mental dissociation from the fear that would normally accompany the ever-present possibility of a real problem. Although the initial reaction to seeing smoke billowing from the control room or hearing water roaring into the engine room might have been raw panic, the drills instilled the fastest possible response to each type of disaster without potentially fatal hesitation. Finally, the drills kept all of us from getting complacent; instead of expecting the equipment to work properly (as it usually did), we came to expect things to go wrong. In future months, when some of the *Viperfish's* systems did malfunction, our automatic responses learned during the drills would help to save us from disaster.

After the flooding drill, I decided that my next step should be to learn everything possible about the boat's emergency escape chamber. Before the next flooding drill or, even more important, in case of a real disaster, I should be qualified on the only system that allowed escape if we were unable to surface. The escape chamber was located in the hangar compartment, where the civilians were–the compartment with the biggest hole. Ironically, the huge hangar was the only compartment that could take on so much water (in the event of a flooding disaster) that the submarine would become too heavy to surface. If it flooded and completely filled with water, there would be no way for any of us to escape.

I caught Chief Mathews as he came off watch in the control room.

"Chief, would you run me through the emergency escape chamber?" I asked.

"That flooding drill get to you, Dunham?"

"No problem," I lied. "Just thought this would be a good time to learn–it's the next system on my quals list."

He looked at my list. "It's one of the next systems. All right, let's look it over."

When we were inside the hangar, we stood below the escape chamber. It was a large, juglike steel structure attached to the overhead escape hatch that connected to the outside of the boat. A ladder extended from the passageway to an opening at the base of the chamber. Paul and I climbed up the ladder and into the chamber while he explained its operation. The interior of the chamber was crammed with valves and pipes, and it took him about fifteen minutes to explain the proper sequence of opening valves to attain pressure equal to that of the surrounding ocean. When the pressures matched, the chamber hatch could then be opened and one could escape from the *Viperfish*.

"Remember your free–ascent training in submarine school, Dunham?" he asked.

"Fifty feet, blow and go," I said. "I remember it well."

Successful ascent up the top half of a hundred–foot tower of water was a requirement for graduation from submarine school. Placed in the middle of the tower (through a special entry chamber that allowed access) without pressurized oxygen or other breathing equipment, the students were told to blow out the air from their lungs as they floated upward toward a tiny circle of light fifty feet above their heads. Being so deep underwater without air tended to focus attention on the immediate matter of survival. If anyone panicked and did not exhale air as he floated toward the circle above, a diving bell holding a bubble of air was dropped down to enclose the man's head. An instructor then blasted the student with one final minute of intense lecturing. If he panicked again, the hapless student was promptly flunked out of submarine school.

"Correct, fifty feet for the sub school students, one hundred feet for the divers. Blow and go! Excellent training for doing exactly the same thing from the *Viperfish*, if the opportunity ever arises." The chief pointed to an opening at the top of the escape chamber that allowed an exit from the boat. "If the boat sinks, do the right things with the valves, climb right through that hole, and you're on your way to the surface."

After we reviewed the sequence of valve operations again and discussed potential problems, the chief said that there was nothing else to learn about escaping and I was now ready to have the system checked off by one of the other crew members.

"By the way," I called out to him after leaving the chamber, "how far down would we descend, if there was flooding?"

He turned around and smiled. "If we sank to the bottom?"

"If we had a leak and sank to the bottom during our trip to Seattle."

After considering the question, he said slowly, "I just talked to the navigator. About an hour ago, we passed well south of the Mendelssohn Seamount and moved into the mid–Pacific. It's a little more shallow back there, but–"

"How shallow is the top of the Mendelssohn Seamount?"

"Oh, somewhere close to fifteen thousand feet."

I stared at the chief.

"A little less," he said, without expression. "It gets deeper during the next couple of days, dropping down to about twenty thousand feet before we finally reach the Juan de Fuca Ridge."

"Chief, our crush depth is–"

"I know all about our crush depth, Dunham. Best thing to do is not spend too much time thinking about the escape chamber."

For the first time since reporting on board the submarine, I fully realized that we could never escape the pressures waiting for us below if we became disabled and sank anywhere in the Pacific Ocean. Our craft could not survive any accidents that destroyed the lifesaving buoyancy of our submarine. There could be no safe landings, no settling on terrain spanning the harsh ocean bottom, no escape for any of us if flooding took us down. During the remainder of the trip, the *Viperfish* seemed to become more confining and our claustrophobia intensified as we each worked to conquer our own fears inside the steel machine that we called our home.

5

THE SEA BAT AND OTHER CREATURES

IN THE NORTHEAST CORNER of the Sea of Japan, the city of Vladivostok stands like an amphitheater, with its center stage of Peter the Great Bay (zaliv Petra Velikogo) near the Sino–Soviet border. During the 1920s, V. I. Lenin had acknowledged the city's enormous distance from the center of the emerging Soviet Union, but he supported its obvious strategic importance as its population increased, finally exceeding 400,000 by 1965.

Although the city was an industrial center in its own right, proximity to the sea provided for its growth and sustenance and led to the building of deep–water moorings, construction of new freight warehouses during the early 1960s, and, finally, development of nuclear weapons storage and support facilities. Further, the seaport's geographic location offered the Soviet Union a gateway to the Pacific and increased the military significance of Vladivostok, as ships and submarines of the Soviet Navy traversed the Sea of Japan. The pride of the Soviet Navy by 1965, the seaport was a thriving east coast military facility because of its year–round accessibility through the Kuril Island choke points to the north–

69

east and the Strait of Korea to the south. Connected by air and rail
links directly to Moscow, Vladivostok allowed the Soviet Navy to
expand its extensive Eastern Fleet and to prepare nuclear missile
–carrying submarines for their journeys across the far waters of the
Pacific Ocean in the direction of the United States.

Protests against U.S. military involvement in Vietnam expanded
in January 1967 when government authorities revealed that, to
date, nearly six hundred U.S. aircraft had been destroyed during
the course of the war. On 31 January, thousands of people repre-
senting the New York–based Committee of Clergy and Laymen
Concerned about Vietnam conducted a protest march before the
White House in Washington, D.C., and demanded a de-escalation
of the war. Approximately two hundred members of a fundamen-
talist Protestant group simultaneously staged a counterdemon-
stration in support of the war.

The intensity of protests increased as religious representatives
and students across the country, from San Francisco to Harvard
University in Massachusetts, staged demonstrations and made
speeches against the war. During this time, the United States
began launching artillery attacks on targets in North Vietnam,
while simultaneously mining rivers north of the DMZ.

On 16 March 1967, President Johnson signed a bill authorizing
$4.5 billion in supplemental funds for the war. Soon thereafter,
Director of Selective Service Lt. Gen. Lewis B. Hershey and
Secretary of Defense Robert S. McNamara announced a new lot-
tery draft system for calling up men into military service, abol-
ished the previously established deferments of graduate students,
and changed the rules so as to draft nineteen–year–olds first.

U.S. government sources announced on 30 March that a record
274 Americans had been killed in Vietnam during the week of 19
March. This raised total combat fatalities to more than 8,560.

On 10 May, the United States and the Soviet Union sent vigorous protests and counterprotests to each other after a "brush–by"
(near–collision) incident between the Soviet destroyer *Besslednyi*
and the U.S. destroyer *Walker* during antisubmarine maneuvers in

the Sea of Japan, 375 miles east of the Soviet port of Vladivostok. Accusing the USSR of harassment, the U.S. Defense Department charged that the Soviet destroyer had engaged in a "dangerous performance" in violation of the international rules of the sea.

▼

BY THE TIME THE *VIPERFISH* reached the mid–Pacific, we had managed to survive fires, floodings, reactor shutdowns, loss of electrical power, and every other condition that Captain Gillon could create to test our response capabilities. Within a kaleido-scope of activity, our lives cycled from quiet sleep in the stillness of our strange, peaceful world of seemingly motionless suspension to sudden jumping and running as loudspeakers blasted out the next disaster. What we rookies did not know, we learned through repe-tition and painful experience, mixed with a continuous barrage of instructions from the qualified men telling us what to do if flood-ing or fires should threaten our underwater existence.

The process of creating drills required considerable ingenuity by the veteran chiefs. A proper drill had to carry maximum men-tal impact and demand the most rapid action in the shortest period of time. This was usually accomplished by generating a mind–numbing pattern of flooding water, billowing smoke, or destructive noises. Other effects, such as men hollering, lights going out, turbines screeching to a halt, and loudspeakers blaring calls for emergency surfacing, all added to the perceived success of the drill.

One of the most frightening drills, besides those that made us think we were going to sink or blow up, was the steam–leak drill. Steam was necessary to drive the turbines, which, in turn, gener-ated electricity and propulsion power. Extremely hot, high–pres-sure steam was called "live steam," widely considered to be unbe-lievably nasty stuff if it ever came into contact with human skin.

Our first steam–leak drill was, of course, impressively realistic, complete with loudspeakers announcing, "Steam leak! Steam leak in the engine room!" and lights going out as various turbines suddenly shut down. I had been studying our ship's SINS (ship's inertial navigation system) in the midships section when the "leak" started. By the time I had raced through the tunnel into the engine room, everybody was hollering directions and the air was filled with steam. More lights went out and then rapidly flashed on again, as the electricians tried to maintain electrical power with falling steam pressure. Our hospital corpsman, a tall black man named Baldridge, whom we called "Doc," stood in the middle of the misty surrealistic scene with a steam suit in hand.

Since reporting on board, I had worried about Doc Baldridge. We all trusted him, but we were concerned about the potential for serious medical problems, such as a surgical emergency, and what he might do to us while waiting for backup. He had placed a big operating room light over one of our dining room tables in readiness for cutting, and I had thanked God a thousand times that my appendix had been removed when I was a child. Theoretically, if any major surgical problems did occur, we would surface and a helicopter or surface craft would provide quick access to medical doctors and a more comprehensive health care system than we had on the *Viperfish*. We all knew, however, that we probably would be unable to surface during the operation of our secret mission.

"This is the steam suit, Dunham," Doc Baldridge hollered. "Put it on, and you can find the leak."

The thing looked like thermal underwear, several inches thick, with a reflective aluminum–type exterior coating and a tiny plastic viewing port. I struggled my way into the suit and tried to see out the viewing port, but it was opaque from the steam of my body. Although I heard the whooshing sound of air being pumped into the suit from somewhere, I felt like I would probably have a heat stroke before I could find any steam leak. With the hood of the suit pulled down tightly over my head, I could hear the faraway muffled voice of Doc Baldridge yelling, "Find the steam leak!"

A gigantic "Michelin–Man," with my thick arms sticking out at thirty–degree angles, I grunted and hobbled down the upper–level engine-room corridor. Feeling like I was suffocating, I slowly rotated my body to the left and right. I looked for the source of steam but could see nothing more than the clouded inside of the visor.

"I can't see anything!" I hollered. My voice, trapped within the suit, echoed off the layers of insulation surrounding me.

"I can't see anything!" I shrieked again and wondered what would happen to my face if I took off the hood in an area of live steam. I turned and looked back up the passageway for Doc Baldridge. As I tried to hold my breath to minimize the fogging, I felt a rising sensation of claustrophobia and suffocation.

Cursing the steam, I finally ripped the hood from my head. I fully expected my face to fry in a blast of searing live steam. Instead, I saw a peaceful, business–as–usual engine room, everything humming along, with no steam or other unnatural disasters.

The loudspeaker blared, "Now, secure from steam–leak drill." I climbed out of the steam suit and tracked down Doc Baldridge.

"Any questions about the steam suit?" he asked, grinning his delight at the sight of my hair matted with sweat and steam moisture.

"How am I supposed to save anybody when I can't see anything?" I asked.

His grin faded. "You couldn't see through the viewing port?"

"Fogged over."

"But we were pumping compressed air into the suit."

"It didn't work, Doc. I couldn't have saved myself, much less anybody else. Do you want to try it?"

A half hour later, Doc had replaced the broken connector at the back of the suit. Our ability to save lives in the event of a real steam leak was now considerably enhanced. Of more practical significance for that moment, however, was that another signature appeared on my qualifications card and I had moved another increment closer to receiving my dolphins.

The drills finally diminished in frequency, and I began to settle into the routine of being at sea. Every twelve hours, I climbed through the tunnel and stood my engine–room watch in front of the large propulsion throttle wheels. After each watch, I was busy with further sessions of studying schematics or reviewing systems with qualified crew members. A couple of times each day, I attempted to take a quick nap before another drill dropped on us. It was physically impossible to sleep for more than three or four hours at a time. During those days, I learned the true value of strong, black Navy coffee.

Among the crew, I discovered numerous subsets of men scattered throughout the boat. Depending on qualification status; time on board; type of work performed; and whether officer, enlisted man, or civilian, each man, of course, was unique. The *Viperfish* contained a menagerie of men with a pecking order defined by military protocol–Captain Gillon at the top and the rookies (non–qual pukes) at the bottom. The civilian scientists, always busy with their project in the hangar compartment, were located somewhere in the middle, I guessed at the time, possibly closer to the top than the bottom.

Although I was a rookie, a green nonqualified enlisted man with nothing to contribute as I learned the ways of the *Viperfish*, I was never made to feel inconsequential. As an emerging nuclear reactor operator, I was acknowledged to be an essential part of the upcoming mission. Reactor operator Randy Nicholson would finish his six–year service in the Navy within a few months, and he seemed driven to show me everything he knew about the *Viperfish*'s reactor system before he left. Like the other men of the crew, he repeatedly emphasized the importance of teamwork to the success of any mission that lay ahead. From the cook in the galley to the nuclear engineering officer in the engine room, from the scientist in the hangar compartment to the seaman blowing the head, every member of the team was essential to the mission, and Nicholson never let me forget it.

Occasionally, light moments broke the tension of drills and the grind of qualifications. About two–thirds of the way across the Pacific Ocean, for instance, we were deeply submerged and gliding nearly twenty thousand feet above the Pioneer Fracture Zone when the voice of Paul Mathews emerged from the loudspeakers.

I had just climbed into my rack for a couple of hours' sleep when my eyes popped open at his announcement.

"Now, attention all hands!" he said authoritatively over the loudspeakers. "A full-grown sea bat has just been isolated from the number two torpedo tube. It is contained, and it is now on display in the hangar compartment."

Jerking the curtain away from the front of my rack, I looked down the dark passageway in the general direction of the hangar. I had heard of fish caught in different sections of our superstructure during previous runs, but a sea bat was something entirely new—*and caught in the torpedo tube?*

I tried to recall the structure of the *Viperfish*'s torpedo tubes. The forward bulkheads at the front end of the hangar compartment contained a total of four torpedo tubes, each twenty-one inches in diameter. I thought it amazing that the bat-thing from the sea, whatever the creature might look like, had somehow become sucked into one of the tubes and even more amazing that the torpedomen were able to capture it. Almost everything I had seen on the *Viperfish* so far was relatively amazing, however, and this event didn't seem that much different. As such, I decided, it must be important enough to investigate.

As I hiked up to the hangar compartment, I wondered why the other men on the boat seemed to be showing remarkably little interest in this creature of the sea. I climbed through the watertight door into the hangar and passed the civilians and Lieutenant Dobkin, all apparently oblivious to the extraordinary event just a few feet away.

Near the forward segment of the *Viperfish*, where the torpedo tubes filled the bulkhead, Spike Norstrum, one of the larger torpedomen, stood next to a black plastic bucket. Water had splashed on the deck around the bucket. Norstrum closely watched the bucket; he was obviously guarding the creature in it.

"Hello, Spike," I said, trying not to divert his attention from his hostage. "I just heard the announcement from Chief Mathews. Is the thing still in the bucket?" I peered into the dark water.

Norstrum grimaced and said, "Can you believe it? I've been on boats for fifteen years, and I have never seen one until today." He frowned and added, "The thing is still in there, but its kinda hard to see since the light is so dim up here. I'm just waiting for Mr. Vogel to tell us what to do with it." He was referring to Peter Vogel, our fire-control officer.

The surface of the water vibrated some, partly because the hull was shaking from the propulsion action of the screws and partly, I was sure, from the movements of the creature.

"Is it still alive?" I asked.

"I think so, although the water hasn't moved much lately." Norstrum narrowed his eyes and studied the bucket.

"Do you have a flashlight, Spike?" I asked, straining to see down into the bucket. I wondered whether the bat would jump out at me if I shined light into its new home. The forward end of the compartment near the torpedo tubes was nearly dark, the light blocked by the torpedoes stacked everywhere around us.

"Here's a light," Norstrum said, producing a tiny penlight with a dim yellow light. "It's not real bright, but it should give you a good feel for the thing." I thought I saw a trace of a smile flash across Spike's face.

I turned on the light and pointed the beam down into the bucket's dark interior. Most of the light reflected off the surface of the vibrating water; I stepped closer to the bucket and leaned over to gain a closer look. Down in the depths of the water, I thought I saw something dark at the bottom, something that was still alive. I leaned closer and strained to see if the dark shape was making any movement.

The plastic baseball bat bounced off my hind end with a loud whack at exactly the moment I realized the bucket contained only water. I emitted a surprised holler as the flashlight flew from my hand and crashed against one of the torpedo tubes. Six or seven men immediately emerged from dark hiding places around us, all of them laughing and joining with Spike Norstrum as they hollered together, "The sea bat gotcha, you non-qual puke!"

As I rubbed my hind end and acknowledged that I was now qualified in Sea Bats 101A, one of the civilians at the other end of the hangar hollered, "Here comes another one!" As the watertight door slammed shut, everybody in the compartment disappeared as quickly as they had appeared, leaving Spike Norstrum and me standing alone next to the bucket. The plastic bat disappeared behind one of the panels near Spike just before we heard the voice of the next victim.

"Where's this sea bat thing?" Richard Daniels's voice boomed across the compartment. "Is it still alive?"

I picked up the flashlight from the deck and headed aft.

"Helluva thing, Richard," I said, shaking my head and pointing my thumb back in the direction of the bucket. "I've never seen anything like it. Here, this flashlight will help give you a better look. It's amazing–"

"Thanks, Rog," he said with so much sincerity that I felt a brief flash of guilt. The last thing I heard before I quickly exited the compartment was Daniels asking Spike curious questions about the nature of this remarkable creature called a sea bat.

For the next several days, I studied the Viperfish torpedo tubes, the firing control system, and everything I could find about torpedoes. I read books on the subject, studied the fire–control panels, and listened to officers and enlisted men describe details of the complex system. I learned about inner doors and outer doors and the improbability of anything from the sea ever getting into the tubes. Finally, Norstrum quizzed me and signed my qualifications card, which indicated that I was now qualified on the *Viperfish* torpedo fire control system–including everything there was to know about sea bats.

At the end of our submerged cruise we broke through the surface of the frigid, glassy–smooth ocean off the forested coast of Washington and quietly glided up the Strait of Juan de Fuca toward the Navy port at Bremerton. Several of us scrambled up the ladder to take advantage of the view from the large flat deck. The morning air was crisp and cold; the skies were a clear blue.

Even though we had been submerged for less than two weeks, the fresh air was invigorating and refreshing, in sharp contrast to the steamy, oil-laden atmosphere within the confines of our boat, especially in the engine room.

As Captain Gillon, the lookouts, and the officer of the deck watched from the top of our sail, the *Viperfish* progressed up the strait. Those of us topside wandered around the deck in our heavy foul-weather coats and took in the scenery on either side of the boat. Peering into the forests, we searched for bears, waving girls, or anything else of interest.

The skyline of Seattle loomed in the distance, a memory passed through my mind of my father's telling me about my great-grandfather when he had entered Seattle from the east one hundred years ago. His covered wagon had passed through freezing snow-clogged passes near Mount Rainier. He had been a man filled with hope, my father said, as he challenged the forces of nature and planned for the future during his long trip to Seattle.

I would tell my father, in a quiet moment long after my years on the *Viperfish* were finished, about that pioneer's great-grandson approaching Seattle from the opposite direction exactly one hundred years later. The man of the newer generation was only twenty-one years of age. He was riding over the cold ocean waters on a nuclear submarine with a top secret project, and he also was filled with hope as he challenged other forces of nature and prepared for the future.

The people of Washington were good to sailors, I discovered the next day. I left the *Viperfish* on a sight-seeing liberty excursion and, wearing my Navy blues and sailor hat, hitchhiked from Bremerton halfway to Portland and then back north again into Seattle. Cars almost crashed into each other as their drivers eagerly pulled over to help me reach my destination.

One driver, a rustic fellow in an old jalopy, elaborately introduced me to his daughter in the backseat as soon as I climbed in the front and shut the door. Feeling like some kind of celebrity, I turned and smiled at the attractive girl. My enthusiasm immediately waned, however, when I discovered that her mother, a large and muscular woman with a mean look, was sitting next to her like a bulldog guard. On close inspection, I realized that the girl was only about fourteen years old. She was chewing on a massive wad of bubble gum and, for the next ten minutes, babbled nonstop. As she rambled on, occasionally blowing monster bubbles that popped with a crack, I mentally changed my destination to the next convenient spot for pulling over. I jumped out of the car and thanked them for their kindness. They waved and rumbled off down the road–the father erratically steering the clunker, the mother flexing her muscles and guarding the daughter, and the pixie girl herself talking and chewing, and chewing and talking, all the while picking globs of pink gum from her hair.

I reached a Seattle enlisted man's club late in the day, ate dinner, and gathered together with some of the *Viperfish* crew who had also discovered the place. We danced with a few of the local ladies (none of whom chewed gum), and, assisted by several cans of cold Olympia beer, blew off steam late into the night before riding the final ferryboat back to Bremerton and the *Viperfish*.

During the next week, we performed more tests in the waters near Bremerton and prepared the *Viperfish* to interact safely with other American submarines in the Pacific Fleet. There wasn't much for me to do except continue with qualifications, stand my watch in front of the throttle wheels, and listen to the stories of my shipmates' exploits in Seattle, each tale becoming more incredible with the passage of time. When we left Puget Sound and sailed in the direction of San Francisco a week later, Marc Birken and I sat in the engine room and hollered our stories back and forth over the whine of the turbines.

"God, she was beautiful!" Marc said, his face lighting up with enthusiasm.

"What was the best part of her, bruddah?" I yelled back.

"Her lips!"

"Her lips?"

"They were fantastic! They were strangely shaped, like nothing I've seen or felt before. They were hot, they..."

He paused and looked at me. "But what about the gal you met?" he asked. "Didn't you say she was young and beautiful?"

"Ah yes. She was not just beautiful, she was spectacular! In the back of a farmer's car, of all places, the finest young lady in all of Washington."

"Where was the farmer?"

"He introduced us! Can you believe that?"

"And you did it with him watching? Right there, in the backseat of his car?"

"Of course, he wasn't watching! He was with his...uh wife, checking out his crops. I'd say she was about nineteen, and we had the car to ourselves!"

Marc grinned, his mind racing. "Silent and sweet, huh?"

"Sweet for sure. Silent? Nope, she talked every minute!"

"I love the talkers," Marc interjected. "My girl, strange lips and all, talked just the right amount, talked and kissed, and she said things I never heard before!"

And so the conversations went, buzzing back and forth across the *Viperfish*, stories upon stories, expanding and making us all seem almost superhuman until nobody was quite sure what to believe.

Passing by the coast of Oregon at periscope depth, we took "periscope liberty" and lined up the scope's cross hairs on the beautiful and rugged coastline on our port side. The scenery took on a surreal quality as the *Viperfish* drifted along at eight knots and our antennae delivered the musical sounds of a coastal radio station into the speakers of the control center. By the end of the day, when we had dropped our periscopes, dived three hundred feet, and aligned our SINS for San Francisco Bay, the stories of conquests faded back into our imaginations where most of them had originated in the first place.

A couple of days later, the dark gray hull of the *Viperfish* emerged from the wall of fog stretching like a curtain across San

Francisco Bay from Mount Tamalpais to Point Lobos. As we cruised across the wind-whipped waters below the Golden Gate Bridge, Captain Gillon allowed those of us not on watch to climb topside to view the spectacular scenery of the bay area. We mingled back and forth behind the bat-cave hump and looked up at the tourists on the bridge who were watching us.

We appeared, I am sure, to be one of the strangest collection of people ever seen on board any military vessel entering the bay. Doc Baldridge wore a straw hat with FREEDOM across the hatband, while most of the men strolling in front of the sail wore the dark-blue lintless "faboomer suits" or the standard Navy dungaree uniforms. The civilians wore various items of clothing that showed little indication of any military connection or their significance on board the *Viperfish*.

Looking around at the tourists on boats passing by, I had a perverse sense of pride in our general appearance of disorder. Contrasting with surface Navy vessels that enter heavily populated harbors with enlisted men standing like statues along the boundaries of their ship, we were a definite contrast. Nobody on our deck stood the right distance from anyone or anything—we just wandered around on the superstructure as we looked at the sights and avoided falling into the bay. In spite of our apparent disorganization, we had a strong sense of pride in our boat and in ourselves. We felt it unnecessary to convince anybody of our capabilities; the substance of the *Viperfish* crew counted, not the show. We were *submariners*, by God, and if people looking at us didn't like the way we looked, we really didn't care.

We passed between Alcatraz Island and Angel Island, made a left turn toward San Pablo Bay, and finally tied up at the Mare Island Naval Shipyard near Vallejo. Because I was on schedule with the qualifications program, Bruce Rossi actually gave me a couple of days away from the boat during scheduled repair work on the *Viperfish*'s nuclear instrumentation.

I caught the first cab to Oakland International Airport and quickly picked up a standby ticket for a flight to Burbank. An hour later, I was home in Glendale where, unannounced, I rang our doorbell and surprised my parents for a weekend visit.

If they had any worries about their son traveling around the ocean in a submarine, they didn't say much about it and I gave them as much reassurance as I could. They showed me a *National Geographic* magazine article about the USS *Skate* pushing up through the ice of the North Pole in 1959. We all looked at the pictures together, while I explained how safe I was during our submerged operations.

Dinner was somewhat of a somber affair. We discussed the expanding Vietnam War; the disruptions in our society because of the war; and the emerging involvement of my younger brother, who was still in high school, with the antiwar movement.

Unfortunately, the family's sleep was interrupted that night by my terror-filled screams during a nightmare about jagged spears of ice pushing through the *Viperfish* pressure hull during patrol under the North Pole.

"It was just a dream," I told them as they rushed into my room. "There is nothing to worry about. We have the best men in the Navy serving on board the *Viperfish*, it is the best ship in the Navy, we're not going under any ice, and we're not going to do any-thing that could be risky. We are a safe submarine and everything will be fine."

The next day, when they questioned me about the future of the *Viperfish* in the months and years ahead, all I could say was that we would be at sea; there could be no further answers until our mission was finished and maybe not even then. I could see the fear and worry in their eyes, especially in my mother's, as the cab arrived and I waved good-by. Their concerns were directed as much toward the unknown dangers in their son's future as to the obvious hazards already present. This torment was known to the families of servicemen everywhere. For my parents, it would not end until we surfaced the final time, when my duty on board the *Viperfish* reached a successful conclusion.

Before returning to the *Viperfish* from the Oakland airport, I requested that the cab driver take me to a student bookstore near the University of California at Berkeley. I needed some books for the chemistry and French college–prep correspondence courses that I had started. Several years before, I had been at the university to watch a Cal–Navy game, and I recalled that the students had been an active, albeit interesting, group of people. I should have taken a clue from the cabby, a wiry little man with a twitching mustache, when he turned to face me after we pulled up to the bookstore.

"Are you sure you want to go in there?" he asked, his mustache quivering.

I assumed he was worried about my disappearing without paying the fare. "I'll leave my bag here," I told him, "I'll be back in about five minutes."

He looked at me as if I were crazy. "Okay, sailor, it's your choice," he finally said, shrugging his shoulders and turning away.

Puzzled, I climbed out of the cab and joined the throngs of students moving into the store. I was wearing my standard "Class A" Navy uniform, silk black tie in a perfect square knot, shoes shined beneath my bell-bottom dark–blue pants, and white Navy hat properly in place. After finding the textbooks and carrying them to the cashier, I first noticed the looks of hostility from the long–haired students standing in line.

I pulled out my wallet and heard the rumble of obscenities, moving just into earshot. There was no doubt about the object of their scorn. Passing back and forth like a rising caldera of contempt, the words demonstrated the strong sentiments of the students' anger. Their comments were clearly directed at what I represented–the military, the Navy, the men involved with the killing in Southeast Asia.

The student clerk who took my money stared with hostility. Ignoring my outstretched palm, he slowly dropped my change on the counter in a gesture of open defiance.

I gave him a word of thanks that was ignored and gathered my books for a rapid exit. The antagonism followed me from the store. The students stopped to stare at my short hair and clean-shaven face, a palpable fury from a population of people hating the government that didn't listen and the war that wouldn't stop.

I wanted to say that they were wrong, that I was just a guy try-ing to become qualified on a submarine from Hawaii, that I didn't use weapons against anyone, and that I was even working full time to defend their right to dissent. I didn't start any war in Vietnam, I don't deserve your scorn.

The cab driver, accelerating to get me away from Berkeley toward the freeway, moved in and out of traffic in a determined effort to clear the area as quickly as possible. I looked out the window at the groups of long–haired students milling around on the sidewalks of University Avenue. As I felt my own anger at their rejection of everything I believed in, a fire truck, with red lights revolving and siren screaming, sped past us in the opposite direction, toward the university. It was towing a trailer marked "bomb–disposal."

The remainder of the ride back to Vallejo and Mare Island was one of silent gloom. The sentiment against the expanding Vietnam War had reached a level where rational debate was disappearing into a whirlpool of student anger and protest. Minds were becom-ing polarized, radical factions were forming, and open discussion was becoming impossible.

Within the confines of the *Viperfish*, we had our answer to the issue. We believed in the military solution to Vietnam as strongly as the students believed in their peaceful solution. We trusted and believed in the sincerity of our national leaders, although the rea-sons for continuing the battle were changing from defending a country and preventing the "domino effect" to not letting those who had already been killed in battle to have done so in vain. As we observed the riots, civil disobedience, and lawlessness of the protesters, we stopped listening to their rhetoric.

What I could not understand that day, and what none of us on the *Viperfish* could understand during the months that followed, was why everybody in the military should be objects of such scorn. None of us made the government's policy on Vietnam–not the soldiers in Southeast Asia and not the sailors on the *Viperfish*. Our crew became victims of this protest, but American soldiers in

Vietnam became double victims. Not only were they ordered to Vietnam to fight, but they were spat upon for being American soldiers.

Our morale began to drop as a result of the protests and so much dissent from those who apparently were doing nothing for their country. The crew responded to student contempt by generating our own contempt for "the hippies and the freaks" who seemed, each time we saw or heard a news report, to be taking over the society that we were defending.

6

NON-QUAL PUKE

THE LONG-HAIRED Berkeley student was an athlete, lean and well conditioned, and he threw his projectile with precision.

The instant the rock struck the leg of the officer in the front line of advancing deputy sheriffs, the student turned and ran up Durant Avenue to escape. The officer had seen the stone coming and felt the pain of its impact. He immediately broke ranks and took up the chase, his helmet bouncing against his head and forty pounds of guns, ammunition, shield, and bullet-proof vest clattering against his body. He was obese and quickly became fatigued. From the towering structures of the Unit One dorms near College Avenue, hundreds of students hollered a barrage of insults at the officer as they watched the chase move up the street. The athlete moved like a rabbit, while the officer fell farther behind, gasping for air as he struggled beneath his heavy load of equipment.

At that moment, a young freshman engineering student walked up the quiet sidewalk on the north side of College Avenue in the direction of the university. Unaware of the chase progressing in his direction and ignoring the noise from Durant Avenue, he carried a full load of books on subjects relating to his science major. He walked quickly, with his head down and his mind deep in thought.

The athlete rounded the corner and, racing past the engineering student, disappeared up an alley as the deputy sheriff reached the area. The student adjusted his load of books and quickly glanced at his watch—he would be late if he didn't hurry. The only warning of danger was the brief sound of gasping before the nightstick struck the side of the young man's head. His books scattered and blood immediately rushed down his neck onto his clean shirt. He fell to his knees and heard the gasping sound of heavy breathing again as the baton, striking a second time, produced more pain and blood.

The outrage and obscenities screamed by the students looking down from the windows of Freeborn Hall were ignored by the officer and unheard by the injured student. He finally collapsed on the asphalt and slipped into a coma.

At this same time, in the waters of the base at Vladivostok, a special class of Soviet submarines loaded 9,000–pound N–3 Shaddock cruise missiles into their launching systems. These winged projectiles, tucked down inside the submarine hull, were designed to be carried away from the vessel by two booster rockets that were quickly jettisoned after the launch. The Shaddock was propelled by a powerful ramjet engine to a speed as high as Mach 2 (twice the speed of sound); the direction to its target was guided and corrected by the submarine's radar system, referred to as Front Piece and Front Door.

The submarine class that carried this missile was known in the Western world as the Echo I fleet submarine. Built by the Soviet Navy to follow the November class developed in 1958 and using an identical nuclear propulsion system, the Echo I was designed with a longer hull that supported three pairs of missile–launching systems. An enlarged version of this submarine, called the Echo II, was built between 1961 and 1967; she was able to launch four pairs of missiles.

During this time, an advanced SS–N–12 missile, weighing 11,000 pounds, was developed with an improved range of nearly three hundred miles. Programmed to follow a supersonic trajectory that hugged the ocean, this lethal missile never reached an altitude of more than 2,200 feet. It was guided by precision radar and satellite missile-targeting systems. All SS–N–12 devices could be launched from the Echo II boats within twenty minutes of their surfacing and could deliver to their targets a deadly barrage of high explosives or nuclear warheads.

▼

RANDY NICHOLSON BROUGHT THE *VIPERFISH* nuclear reactor on line early that morning in 1967. By 0800, we had stationed the maneuvering watch and were progressing down the Napa River in the direction of San Pablo and San Francisco Bay. We passed the distant campanile tower at the University of California, Berkeley, on our port bow before we finally turned right and plowed through the whitecaps toward the Golden Gate Bridge. Jim McGinn and I sat in the back of the engine room and held the throttle wheels while we listened to the loudspeaker commands from Lieutenant Katz, who was standing watch as the OOD at the top of our sail. It was a gloomy day topside, wet and cold, and nobody ventured up to catch the freezing wind and watch the fog pass by.

After traversing the waters below the Golden Gate Bridge and continuing into the Pacific Ocean, it came as almost a blessing for us finally to clear the bridge and submerge, down and away from the miserable day above. The men standing watch in the control center established the usual down–angle as the *Viperfish* descended several hundred feet into the silent water, leveled her off, and set a course for the Hawaiian Islands, three thousand miles away.

About this time, Bruce Rossi began to intensify the pressure on me to become qualified on the nuclear control systems. Several of the nuclear-trained men, in addition to my mentor, Randy Nicholson, would be leaving the Navy shortly after we reached

Pearl Harbor, and the training of their replacements was essential for the continued operation of the *Viperfish*.

"Are you working on your engine–room qualifications?" Rossi asked me that first afternoon out, shortly after I left my watch station at the throttles.

I pulled out my qualifications card and handed it to him. "In two or three more days, I'll be finished with the sanitary tanks and the..."

His jaw muscles pulsating vigorously, he glared at my card, mottled with coffee spots, greasy fingerprints, and blotches of oil from various systems. "You're doing fine with the ship's qualifications, but we need you in the engine room. Finish the sanitary tanks today, along with these other auxiliary systems awaiting final signature, and get to work on the nuclear systems."

"But what about all these other systems?"

"You'll have time for them later, Dunham," he said. "We need you qualified in the engine room, or Nicholson will have to start goddamn port–and–starboard watches."

He thrust the card back at me and, with a look like he was getting ready to shoot somebody, huffed away in the direction of the engine room. It was a challenge to be enclosed in the submarine with somebody like Rossi storming back and forth, tightening the screws, pushing and pushing. There would be no escape from his twenty–four–hour surveillance. He would be watching me, asking me, occasionally encouraging me, but always pushing. The mandate was clear: get qualified on the reactor systems, and do it before the *Viperfish* runs short of qualified watchstanders. Avoid the goddamn port–and–starboard watches for anybody.

Everybody was feeling the pressure, now that we had almost finished the trial runs to test the crew and equipment. The evaluation of our Special Project was now rapidly looming, but the scientists on board would be able to do little with their Fish without an adequate number of qualified nukes. I stared at my card, one whole side of it without signatures next to such items as the nuclear reactor, the primary and secondary nuclear shielding systems, the steam generator systems, the condensers, the feed pumps, the primary coolant pumps, and all the associated electronics that allowed for the safe operation of the equipment. I looked down the passageway at Bruce, his thick arms vigorously gesturing while he talked to Richard Daniels, and I got to work.

Two hours later, I knew everything any reasonable man could ask about the sanitary tanks. I even knew how to blow them, if necessary, and a couple of the forward crew signed off the requirement. I then gathered every technical manual I could find relating to nuclear reactor operations and found a quiet corner in the engine room to begin the process of learning everything I could about how power was generated on the *Viperfish*.

It was becoming clear that before I would finish all the qualifications on board the boat and actually start standing reactor operator watches–contributing something back to the Navy–I would have been in the service almost four years. The process of training seemed to last forever.

The complexity of nuclear power operations, especially on board an operational submarine such as the *Viperfish*, mandated a long training program. Although it might seem that a college degree would be necessary for any man to be considered for the nuclear power program, I discovered early in my Navy career that this was not the case. To the contrary, one of the most remarkable things about the men of the nuclear program was how many had flunked out of college before joining the Navy. I would have found this even more amazing except for the fact that, before joining the Navy, I too had been asked not to enroll for the semester following my first year of college.

I came into the Navy lost and impressionable.

The Navy is quite good at finding dropouts with the potential for learning the volume of technical information necessary for the safe operation of a nuclear power plant. The search for such men could have enormous consequences because placing them in the nuclear program is a high-stakes gamble. The Navy, effectively, is betting that they can successfully finish the long years of nuclear training and eventually be able to operate a complex reactor system safely, in spite of their previous academic records.

For me, the process began in 1963 at the U.S. Navy recruiting office in Pasadena, California. I had wandered there shortly after receiving a letter, from the Glendale Junior College administration office, informing me that because of my abysmal performance as a student, I no longer could be one.

"I wanna fly jets," I told the pleasant chief petty officer recruiter in a uniform covered with an incredible amount of gold.

"Okay," he answered with a smile, as he studied my nineteen-year-old face. "The Navy can put you in jets, no problem. However, you have to join first and then apply for flight training later. Also, there is no guarantee that you would ever be accepted. How much college training do you have?"

"Oh, about one year," I answered hesitantly, wondering if D's and F's allowed me even to count much of that time. I decided not to tell him that I had talked over the matter of my grades with my parents, and it was at their suggestion that I was standing before him. I also decided not to tell him how much I disliked the long and painfully boring lectures about Chinese objects of art and Plato's concepts of life, which had filled my abysmal college experience. I had felt like I was sitting on a train, with no destination, as I watched the mundane scenery passing by. During my entire freshman year, I could not wait to escape and set my own course, one that would include as much adventure as I could find. Finally, I hoped that the recruiter would not ask any questions about my college grades.

"Good!" he exclaimed. "That's very good! However, the Navy has a special program that allows me to guarantee you, in advance, *before you even sign the papers,* a special training program that is only for intelligent and highly motivated men."

He gave the impression that he was going to share the greatest secret of all time with me. Reaching into his desk, he pulled out a large color picture of a nuclear submarine control center and held it up in front of me. I studied the images of periscopes, the clusters of red and green lights, and the group of enlisted men who looked like they were ready to attack everything in sight.

"You could be a part of this team!" the chief exclaimed excitedly and pulled out a stack of papers. "Just read about this great program. We'll give you a simple test, and we'll soon know if you have what it takes to be guaranteed a future with nuclear power! It is a very challenging program."

I sat down next to his desk. After confirming that I had no interest in either the Communist Party or overthrowing our government, I passed the test, which seemed remarkably simple, with flying colors. Intent on becoming a nuclear-trained submariner, I quickly signed the enlistment papers that obligated me for the next six years of my life. One week later, feeling the challenge of a fresh future and new opportunity for adventure, I boarded a Greyhound bus with six other new enlisted men. In a cloud of black diesel smoke, we headed toward the boot camp at San Diego and wherever that would lead us.

I soon discovered that the real test for nuclear candidates was not given in the recruiter's office but at Camp Nimitz, in between running across acres of asphalt known as "the grinder" and tying square knots. The test was designated the GCT (General Classification Test). Actually, it was an extremely difficult and comprehensive IQ test. If the Navy confirmed that an applicant did have adequate brains, then he moved ahead in the system. On the other hand, if the applicant did badly on the test—well, there is a tiny, seemingly innocuous statement in the previously signed enlistment papers that says something about "the needs of the Navy come first."

"Too bad you didn't do well on the test, sailor, too bad you're not going to get nuclear training, but we can always find a place for your skills, doing manual laborlike things. We have this big ol' aircraft carrier with hundreds of decks that need to be swabbed...."

The new sailor who did extremely well on the test, however, would be, finally, absolutely guaranteed nuclear power training (but not necessarily submarine duty). If he did all these things and was unlucky, he could be assigned to a nuclear surface ship and spend the next several years wondering where, in the long process of taking tests and signing papers, he had gone wrong. For the 3 percent of Navy enlisted men who were very lucky, the ones for whom the "needs of the Navy" matched the desire of the individual, submarine duty would beckon.

During the nearly three years following boot camp, the Navy flew me around the country to one training program after another as I completed courses in electronics and nuclear power. The courses were as tough as anything I would later face at the University of California, Los Angeles, School of Medicine; most important of all, I learned to study, I grew up, and, by the time I started submarine school beneath the dreary clouds of New London, Connecticut, I was fully prepared to become a nuclear star.

As the *Viperfish* moved across the Pacific in the direction of the Hawaiian Islands, I worked day and night to learn the theoretical details of the nuclear propulsion system. While a student in nuclear power school, I had thought the study of nuclear fission and the physics relating to the transfer of heat to steam generators to be relatively uncomplicated. The reactor produces heat; the heat boils the water to create steam; the steam spins a turbine to generate power; and, when the screws begin to churn, the submarine moves through the ocean! The reality of the unique system within the actual submarine was quite different, however, because of the complexities associated with controlling the system and the variances among the many submarines in the fleet. The engine room generated a tremendous amount of heat and power, and with the power came an enormous responsibility of the reactor operator to keep the nuclear genie under control. Also, the feeling of being surrounded by so much raw power, the roaring noise of steam, the screaming of turbines, the pounding of pumps, all in the setting of the vibrating hull from the rotation of the *Viperfish's* powerful screws, tended to focus one's concentration far more than any experience in the classroom.

The pinnacle of the engine-room qualification system was the process of learning to control the nuclear reactor. Locked out of sight under yellow lead glass windows, the reactor required precision control mechanisms to maintain a steady-state nuclear fission process that would produce the right amount of power without overheating or leaking radiation. The design of the entire system was based on extraordinary safety considerations to minimize risks to the men working in the engine room and to the environment. Even with a safe design, however, the need for safe control was continuously hammered into our minds.

The psychological pressure during this time was extreme, not only because of the timetable for qualifications and the continuous pressure from Bruce Rossi, but also because of the enormous responsibilities associated with control of the reactor. For a twenty-one-year-old man, barely three years out of boot camp, who had flunked out of college, just sitting in front of a panel that controlled millions of watts of thermal and nuclear energy driving a propulsion engine with two shafts that delivered six thousand horsepower was, in itself, a most awesome responsibility.

The seat facing the panel was in a cramped area at the back corner of the engine room. When I sat in the chair, I faced hundreds of lights, meters, control switches, and audible alarms that shrieked out various abnormal conditions when a drill was under way and everything seemed to be falling apart. The electrician in charge of all the electricity generated and used throughout the *Viperfish* was also seated in this area (the maneuvering room). As the reactor operator and electrician sat side by side, facing their panels, the engineering officer of the watch (EOOW) sat on the edge of his chair or paced back and forth behind them and watched all of the panels. Working to put everything together, he often hollered orders through the loudspeaker system to other men stationed around the engine room. Next to the

EOOW, squeezed in the same tiny area, was yet another man, the chief of the watch, who also oversaw everything and worked to determine what might be going wrong at any given moment.

In the middle of a typical drill, when the nuclear system seemed to be self–destructing, I soon learned that everybody jumped up from their chairs and stood in front of their panels as they flipped switches and called out information to the EOOW, who, in turn, grabbed his microphone and blasted out orders over the loud-speakers. During all this time, lights throughout the engine room were going out as electrical power was lost; alarms were blasting out their shrill noises; circuit breakers were slamming open or shut; red lights were flashing; and other loudspeakers, controlled by men outside the engine room, were announcing the loss of reactor power. Although appearing to be total chaos, this was actu-ally a tightly coordinated process of highly trained men taking action to allow for the continued production of power. The system worked quite well–most of the time.

Always in the back of my mind was the thought that, if I screw up the reactor in some unexpected manner, if I twitch a switch to the right instead of the left, or if I forget some important fact I had been trained to know, I could conceivably kill us all. It was this fear, plus the intense training always to "make things safe" no mat-ter what disaster might be happening, that led to my nightmare.

We were about halfway to Pearl Harbor and I had squeezed into my rack to catch a couple of hours' sleep before taking the next training reactor operator watch. Just before I went to sleep, the *Viperfish* surfaced and began rolling back and forth. I moved into a deep sleep and envisioned myself sitting before the reactor control panel. Plunging deeper into the dream, I watched the meters and red lights before me as the boat increasingly rolled from the impact of the waves on the hull. With each movement of the boat, the reactor control panel lifted high above my head and then dropped down far below me. Suddenly, we took a huge roll at the moment I was looking up at the reactor control panel tow-ering above me. To my horror, the entire panel broke off its moorings and fell on top of me. It knocked me from my seat and crushed me against the floor!

For an indeterminate period of time, I found myself tightly squeezed under the massive panel as I struggled to "make everything safe," mostly by just trying to shut down the nuclear reactor. The panel crushed my arms and I struggled as hard as I could to reach the SCRAM switch that would shut down the plant. I cursed with the effort, I ground my teeth, I sweat furiously, I stretched my arm as far as possible in the direction of the switch, and I cursed again. Just as I accepted that I was going to die, I woke up.

Trying to orient my mind in the darkness of my rack, I discovered that I had somehow managed to turn myself all the way around, a feat that was almost physically impossible. My head was mashed against the bulkhead where my feet normally rested, my arm was trapped behind the medicine cabinet next to the sleeping area, my dungarees were drenched with sweat, and my head pounded from the clenching of my teeth.

I lay silently in the quiet dark of my rack for ten minutes and tried to assess the stress factors associated with my efforts to become a reactor operator: the lack of sleep, the confined quarters, the repetition of intense drills, Bruce Rossi hammering away about quals, the necessity to get qualified before Nicholson departed the *Viperfish*, the control of so much power upon which all our lives depended. Stress was taking its toll, and the nightmare seemed like a sign that it might be too much for me.

The psychological tests I had taken in submarine school were filled with strange questions about our feelings relating to the odor of a man's sweat, the feelings we would have after launching Polaris missiles, and other feelings about this and that. We had been told that there were "no right answers, no wrong answers." From the unplanned departure of several men from our class immediately after the test was graded, it was apparent that some answers were not right enough to suit the Navy. There was nobody on the *Viperfish* to counsel us about stress, and I would · not have been inclined to meet with a psychiatrist if one had been on board. So, I just pulled my curtain tightly shut and thought the thing through.

After a half hour of contemplation, I finally decided that my reaction to everything so far was, in fact, appropriate to the conditions that I was experiencing. When all hell breaks loose at four hundred feet below the surface, one is *supposed* to react, even start shaking a little, if the reactor develops a SCRAM and the lights go out—so long as the reactions are appropriate and the problems are properly resolved. "Builds character" was a phrase often used when we reflected on the intensity of various drills and our reactions to these challenges. I pushed the nightmare from my mind, climbed back into the engine room, and proceeded to build more character at the reactor control panel of the *Viperfish*.

And that was the night we burned a hole through the movie.

I took a couple of hours off after the evening meal to escape into the Hollywood drama projected against a screen on the far bulkhead of the dining area. It was a low-budget cinema with no plot to speak of, but the dining area was filled to capacity because of one beautiful actress who would provide us, we all hoped, with some memories of what women looked like. Steaming below the Pacific Ocean, surrounded by steel and men and nothing but a few pictures here and there to remind us of the females of our species, we were eager to watch—and to fantasize about—the actress.

When she walked across the screen, she was as beautiful as we remembered, her sweet body looking gorgeous as she moved from one scene to the next. Each time she appeared, conversations among the men hushed as each of us mentally placed ourselves into the movie.

At about the middle of the film, during a bathing scene that showed the actress washing herself from behind an opaque shower door, we all struggled to imagine the details of what we were unable to see. To our delight, she was suddenly called from the shower to answer the telephone, and we were treated to a flash of the naked woman moving at high speed before the camera.

"Stop the movie!" at least five voices hollered in unison as Larry Kanen grabbed the controls of the projector.

"Back it up!"

"Bring her back!"

"Reverse the projector!"

Back up the film, Kanen!"

In a few seconds, Kanen finally found the reverse switch and we were all treated to the scene played backward, the actress flashing before the camera again as she backed into the shower, with water flowing up from the drain into the shower head.

"Look at that body!" one of the machinist mates said.

"Jesus, I'm gonna die!" another exuberant voice called out.

"Make it go forward, *slowly!*" Nicholson hollered from the other side of the dining area.

"I'm working on it, I'm working on it," Kanen said, his voice harassed. "Hang on a second, you bunch of horny bastards."

The shower water began flowing in the correct direction again, and we all leaned forward for a closer look. Kanen moved the film slowly, one frame at a time as we waited and waited. After about five long minutes, we saw the shower door begin to open in slow motion and all of us prepared to savor the moment.

The actress moved halfway out of the shower before we discovered that she was actually clothed in some kind of flesh–colored towel that couldn't be visualized at normal projector speed.

"She has a towel on!" Richard Daniels exclaimed with disappointment.

"They cheated us!" several others moaned.

The frustration could not have been more complete. Kanen chose that moment to slow the movement of the film, finally freezing her in the center of the screen for us to enjoy watching whatever we could see. Suddenly, without warning, the center of the towel began turning a brown–black color from the heat of the projector light. Like a torch, the projector burned a hole right through the image.

"You're burning up the movie!" somebody yelled as we watched the meltdown of our actress.

"Dammit, Kanen, you just fried the lady!" another voice called out, while Kanen cursed and struggled to move the picture ahead at normal speed.

"Sorry, I was doing the best I could," Kanen said. Groups of men left the room in disgust–cursing Hollywood for faked nudity, cursing Kanen for melting the best part of the movie, and cursing the fact that this was the only theater in our submerged town. About half of us remained in our seats and hoped for other scenes that could be supplemented by our imagination. We also felt a little guilty. When the movie was watched by other submariners in other oceans, the most exciting scene would not only be fake, but it would be vaporized.

I returned to my rack later that night and slept peacefully until the next watch in front of the reactor control panel. Free of nightmares, my dreams were filled with beautiful naked women jumping in and out of showers, my sleep was peaceful, and the long process of reaching for dolphins continued without pause.

As we moved closer to Oahu, the training watches in front of the reactor panel continued generating additional disasters that gradually, to my amazement, began to seem almost routine. As I sat in the chair before the wall of meters, red lights, and alarms, it gradually dawned on me that only a limited number of conditions could snarl the system. One engine room, one reactor–how many things could possibly go wrong? Only so many red lights and only a specific number of alarms could blast out warnings of new havoc and destruction. Once each red light or row of red lights had flashed, once the buzzing and screaming alarms had sounded, and once I had shut down the reactor and brought it back on line over and over again, there was not much left to happen. Although I still bolted to my feet when red lights and alarms announced an emerging disaster and still felt the rush of adrenaline and pounding of my heart when the lights in the engine room abruptly went out or the circuit breakers flashed their electrical arcs, my actions started to become more automatic and much less stressful.

A further boost to my increasing confidence occurred during the final days of the training cruise. Randy Nicholson, who always stood behind me in the maneuvering area, actually began to treat me like someone approaching an equal, rather than like a trainee. He encouraged me, rather than directed me, as we plotted courses of action in response to the system failures Rossi and others were throwing at us, and increasingly showed approval of my work. I began to *feel* the reactor system. It was in my mind—all the individual pieces of machinery interrelating and working together—and I began actually to like the work I was doing.

I also discovered that teamwork was as essential to successful operation of the reactor system as it was to so many other activities throughout the *Viperfish*. In the cramped maneuvering room, sitting next to the trainee electrician learning to control his monster of a panel, I learned the strengths and weaknesses of the men around me. Two electricians, the stoic Donald Svedlow and the quiet Brian Lane, watched the electrical panel during the training activities as I watched mine, each of us waiting for the next disaster. If I lost the reactor for any reason, the power for the steam turning their turbogenerators would disappear rapidly; if they lost electricity for any reason, my reactor would not work properly. I gave them power for their electricity, they gave me electricity to control my power—we depended on each other. We learned to synchronize our activities, to warn each other if anything we were doing would clobber whatever the other was doing, and to understand that symbiosis was the essence of submarine duty.

Most important, I had trust in the other men. When Svedlow found his electrical meters going wild and the submarine plunging into darkness, he showed a cool, analytical capability to decide what was going wrong and what could be done to resolve the problem. Often, he didn't even stand up like I always did when everybody was trying to yell above the screaming alarms. He just flipped his switches in the proper sequence, watched the battery come to life, synchronized high-voltage electrical circuits, and slammed circuit breakers open and shut in the right sequence to resolve the problems. Frequently, when he was finished with the awesome display of his efficiency, he leaned back in his chair, made an obtuse joke about something totally unrelated to the *Viperfish*'s operations, and calmly gazed over the rows of meters under his control.

Lane had a different style. Quiet most of the time, he rarely said more than a few words about anything, including the electrical control panel and his wife and children in Honolulu. From time to time, a slow smile crossed his generally passive face, and he always flipped the electrical switches with somewhat less authority than Svedlow. He was a serious man. Nothing seemed to faze him, and he rarely joined in the back-and-forth humor that most of us relied on to keep our sense of perspective. The guy didn't cuss or even chew tobacco, and he didn't carouse or drink much alcohol during our ports of call.

As I moved into the position of running the reactor, the unique personalities among the crew became better known to me. Rossi scared all of us; Chief Jack Morris (one of the veteran electricians) seemed jittery but essentially competent; Lane was the most stable, never reacting much or affected by anything; and Svedlow demonstrated raw capability and authority that impressed everybody.

One hundred miles east of Oahu, we surfaced onto a glassy-smooth, warm ocean and discovered a shark wedged in our superstructure. From the top of the sail, one of the topside watches spotted the dark gray creature flopping around on the deck with one of its fins inside an opening. Larry Kanen volunteered to climb out the door in the side of the sail and free the creature. While keeping his distance from the rows of impressive and amply displayed teeth, he gingerly leveraged it free, with a long steel pole. By the time the shark slid off the *Viperfish* and swam away from us, we were ready to dive again and proceed to Pearl Harbor. Nobody thought of taking a picture of the event, but we speculated that it was probably one of the rare times in the history of submarine operations that a full-sized shark had been briefly taken into captivity by a trolling superstructure.

During the final miles of our submerged voyage from San Francisco, I became aware of my changing perspective about the niceties, the small amenities, that I had always taken for granted before living on the *Viperfish*. Such food substances as milk and fresh vegetables became increasingly less important when they became unavailable after leaving port. Genuine milk (different from the white powdered variety that tasted unlike any milk I had ever consumed) disappeared first, followed by fresh vegetables and fruit. Meals then consisted of canned, frozen, and prepared food retrieved by the cooks from our refrigerators and mammoth dry-storage compartments for each meal. The fruit stored weeks before in my bunk locker was long gone, and the galley had none to replace it.

Showers no longer seemed as necessary. We all had some degree of body odor, and nobody much cared whether or not someone else smelled good. On top of that basic fact, the physical act of taking a submarine shower is not an event to relish. First, the individual takes off all his clothes in the cold head and finds a convenient place to hang the towel. Next, before his feet turn blue on the frigid steel decking (moist with the contents of various drains that bubbled out when the sanitary tank was last blown), he jumps into the metal stall. Ignoring the clusters of men who are taking care of their toilet needs in the crowded stalls around him, he stands naked and freezing below the shower head. With a bar of soap in hand, he bravely turns on the water.

A blast of ice water hits him in the face. Clean water on the *Viperfish* does not come cheaply; every drop is precious. After a quick wetting down, he immediately turns off the water before somebody slaps the side of the stall and yells, "Hey, quit wasting water! Haven't you ever heard of a submarine shower?" Chilled to the bone, he lathers himself and then turns the shower on for a speedy final blast of water (that is finally beginning to warm up) to wash off the soap.

He jumps out of the stall and dries off before pneumonia bacteria can begin their assault on his freezing body. Finally, just before one of the galley crew comes in and hollers, "Everybody out, I'm gonna blow the head!" he flees in the direction of his rack.

The briefest of fantasies probably flirts with his mind: What would it be like to take a real shower, just one long steaming hot shower, at home?

Washing hands before eating was another ritual that faded as we grabbed food before or after standing watch. Working in the engine room, or almost anywhere else throughout the *Viperfish*, resulted in a substantial accumulation of black grease on hands that gripped pipes, turned valves, and flipped switches. The grease was always there–an unwelcome companion, but one that was ignored because of its constant presence. If it was not convenient to wash our hands, we gave them a quick wipe against our dunga-rees before sitting down to eat. This token effort removed the largest clumps of foreign matter that might actually affect the taste of the food.

After leaving the morning watch on the reactor control panel that last day before reaching Pearl Harbor, I discovered we were having sandwiches, make-your-own style, with fresh-baked bread. Each crew member sliced the bread for his own sand-wiches. By the time I reached the table, the loaf on the cutting board was about half gone. The remaining half was considerably darker than the other loaves around it. Closer inspection revealed that a layer of grease had accumulated from the many hands gripping the loaf.

I hesitated briefly, but soon I was sitting with the other men and wolfing down my sandwich. The bread slid easily down my throat, and the greasy grime did not seem to affect the taste to any significant degree.

Sitting next to me at the table was one of our larger nuke shipmates, a man relatively new to the *Viperfish*, who was known as Baby Bobbie. Immediately, I noticed his distinctly strong body odor. Everybody smelled bad, but Baby Bobbie, for some reason, always smelled worse. In fact, he smelled so bad that most of us habitually sat as far away as possible when we found ourselves in his presence. I took another bite of my sandwich and eased a couple of inches away from the man. Of course, I could always disguise his odor by lighting a cigar–a good cloud of cigar smoke always seemed to make any odor acceptable.

That evening, Lt. Comdr. Gerry Young, the *Viperfish*'s engineer, walked me through the engine room, and asked me hundreds of questions about the many pieces of machinery. He seemed happy with my answers and signed off my engineering qualifications card. He then referred me to the captain.

As the commanding officer, Stuart Gillon held the ultimate authority to grant me the privilege of controlling the nuclear reactor on his submarine. Everything that happened on board, whether or not Captain Gillon was directly involved, was his final and absolute responsibility. It was important to him to pay careful attention to the knowledge of the men certified as "qualified." For that reason, I expected an extraordinarily difficult examination about the fine points of reactor operations and the minutiae of the control systems.

He brought me into his office and politely asked me to sit down across from the tiny table attached to the bulkhead. To my immense surprise, we talked philosophy for the next half hour. Speaking in his characteristic soft voice, he encouraged me to remain at the peak of my knowledge about nuclear operations and educated me about the various antinuclear protests working to disrupt operations involving nuclear machinery.

"Some of these people are fanatic about their beliefs," he said, describing various protest movements around the United States. "They are looking for anything they can find that incriminates nuclear power, no matter how far from reason their claims may be. A safe nuclear operating program on the *Viperfish* will help protect the Navy from the claims of these activists."

We talked about the sinking of the *Thresher* and discussed reasons for serving on board submarines. He finally dismissed me with an announcement that there was soon going to be a change in command on board the *Viperfish*. Comdr. Thomas Harris would assume the position of the boat's commanding officer, he said, and would lead the *Viperfish* into the challenges of the mission awaiting us.

At the conclusion of the meeting, I was designated an official reactor operator of the USS *Viperfish*, a title that allowed me the pleasure of standing regular unsupervised watches in front of the reactor panel. No ceremony and not much in the way of congratulations took place. Rather, a simple notation was added to my service record that I was a qualified *Viperfish* reactor operator and I could now stand watches. Unfortunately, I still had another six months of work on the remaining components of the *Viperfish*. before I could achieve the coveted position of being qualified in submarines. Until that distant day of glory arrived, I was still just a non–qual puke who could, incidentally, now run the reactor.

That night, we surfaced several miles off Pearl Harbor. Because I was off watch and had nothing to do, I wandered up to the control center and requested permission to "lay to the bridge." I scrambled up the ladder out of the vessel and then continued to climb another sixty–five feet up to the cockpit at the top of the sail. The two lookouts and the OOD, the nuclear–trained Lieutenant Katz, were standing in the cramped space and looking out at the world around them.

It was a night to empower the soul. The bow of the *Viperfish* hissed through the glassy black waters, a florescent glow enriching the white foam on either side of her. The sea was calm, there was no pitching or rolling, and we seemed to be gliding across a carpet of black velvet. The moonless sky was filled with a spray of stars. Thirty degrees off our port bow, near the horizon, the distant lights of Honolulu summoned us to her promised pleasures. It was almost a surrealistic spectacle, the magic and the beauty further enhanced by the weeks of confinement within the *Viperfish*.

"Got channel fever, Dunham?" Lieutenant Katz finally asked.

"Channel fever, sir?" I vaguely remembered somebody telling me about the condition, a common affliction at the end of a patrol.

"Channel fever," one of the lookouts repeated. "Can't go to sleep, can't slow down, can't think, can't do anything of value."

"You'll feel it more when we've been out longer," Katz said. "A month or two out here and you won't be able to sleep for days before we reach the channel."

"It's like overdosing on about twenty cups of coffee," the lookout said, putting the binoculars to his eyes and studying the distant lights of Honolulu. "It's a chompin' at the bit to get off the boat."

"Haven't had any problem, yet," I said, confidently. "Always able to sleep when the time is available."

After a few more minutes of stars, lights, and florescence, I thanked the three men and left them with their treasure as the *Viperfish* continued to glide across the waters off Oahu. I stood the mid-watch (midnight to 0400) at the reactor panel and later climbed into my rack for some sleep before we entered Pearl Harbor.

For the next four hours, I lay in my tiny dark enclosure and stared at the aluminum sheet metal four inches away from my face. Unable to sleep, I was feeling the excitement in the air and sensing the tone and enthusiasm of the conversations up and down the passageway of the crew's berthing area. The entire crew of the *Viperfish* had channel fever, and the only cure was to enter the waters of Pearl Harbor and go ashore to blow off some steam.

Marc Birken and I sat side by side at the throttle watch as we finally moved up the channel to the submarine base the next morning. Like a couple of excited schoolboys, we both raced up the engine room ladder to the topside deck as the lines were pulled to the pier. Blinking into the bright sunlight, I scanned the crowd of people who had been waiting for our return. Wearing colorful muumuus, wives waved to their husbands as they spotted them climbing from the hatches. Children called to their fathers. A cluster of gold-covered naval officers, in their dress whites, waited to speak with Captain Gillon and the civilian scientists.

I had no reason to expect that anybody would be waiting for me at the pier. My family was in California, I knew almost nobody in Hawaii, and my only friends were the men on board the *Viperfish*. The brow, lowered to the boat, connected the pier to our topside deck, and the men began streaming across it to their loved ones.

"Let's go hit the beach, bruddah," Marc Birken said from my side. His voice sounded different, quieter, his enthusiasm dampened by the same feelings that I was experiencing. Although these feelings were completely illogical, it seemed that after we had been at sea for so many weeks and accomplished all of the tasks set before us, somebody should be waiting for our return.

I turned to Marc and nodded, "It's time to go steaming. You get your miserable shore-power cables connected, and we'll check out what's happening in Waikiki."

Two months later, the scientists on board hoisted two top secret deep-submergence Fish into the hangar spaces of the *Viperfish*, and we began loading garbage weights and food stores in preparation for the tests that lay ahead. Again, there was no information provided about our upcoming mission. There were no briefings about our future, and nothing was said about where in the Pacific Ocean we were going.

The future mission of the *Viperfish* remained a secret to all of the crew.

THE DOLPHINS

PROTESTS AGAINST THE VIETNAM WAR, fueled by the energy of students soon to be eligible for the draft, began to expand during the early months of 1968. Spreading across the country, the turmoil escalated as the civilian population became polarized into "hawks" versus "doves," and the young became alienated against "anybody over the age of thirty." The peace symbol emerged as a protest against Vietnam and all military policies. The hawks promptly ridiculed this clawlike representation and called it the national symbol of the American chicken.

In Vietnam, 7,500 U.S. soldiers were shifted north toward the DMZ to support South Vietnamese Premier Nguyen Ky's efforts to stop the influx of Communist troops. As the Vietcong attacked American troops, protesters in the United States began burning their draft cards. Protesters numbering in excess of 100,000 were led by Rev. Dr. Martin Luther King, Jr.; Stokely Carmichael; and Dr. Benjamin Spock on a protest march from New York's Central Park to the headquarters of the United Nations. Other protesters, sponsored by the Spring Mobilization Committee to End the War in Vietnam and led by

Black Nationalists, later marched in California; 50,000 people heard antiwar speeches at San Francisco's Kezar Stadium by Coretta King, wife of the Reverend Dr. King, and Robert Scheer of *Ramperts* magazine. As protesters urged students across the country to mobilize against the war, J. Edgar Hoover, director of the Federal Bureau of Investigation, reported to President Lyndon B. Johnson the details of "antiwar activity." On NBC–TV, Secretary of State Dean Rusk said, "Communist apparatus is behind the peace movement all over the world and in our own country."

Sea trials for the Soviet's Echo II submarine, conducted in the Sea of Japan and the western Pacific Ocean, tested the new SSGN vessel to its designed test depth of 1,148 feet while working to remain well above its collapse depth of 1,900 feet. The extensive testing program included test firings of twenty–one–inch diameter torpedoes, and putting the FENIKS–M sonar and SNOOP SLAB radar systems through their electronic paces. Although the men serving on board submarines of this class did not know it at the time, their submarines were to become infamous as the most dangerously unsafe class of vessel in the Soviet's nuclear navy, with four serious disasters during the decade ahead. Another major problem for the Echo IIs involved inadequate radiation shielding, which endangered the physical health of the crew. The twin reactor system (designated first–generation HEN reactors) of this class, with its associated increased shielding needs, further magnified the dangers to the crew as a result of excessive doses of neutron and gamma radiation. This issue was brought into harsh focus when the Soviets made the shocking discovery that their "dirty" (high–radiation emitter) boats actually could be tracked by surface craft designed to detect the "radiation wake" of the submerged submarines.

▼

AFTER COMPLETING OUR SHAKEDOWN CRUISE to the West Coast, several fundamental changes occurred on the *Viperfish*. The first and most significant of these was to welcome on board the new captain of the *Viperfish*, Comdr. Thomas Harris.

All of us were used to change–of–command ceremonies on board the *Viperfish*. Whenever anybody of prominence moved in or out of the submarine base command structure, our boat was chosen as background scenery for the ceremony. The reason for this tradition apparently related more to our substantial deck space than to anything we offered as a submarine. Although the ceremonies were generally conducted on the pier next to the *Viperfish*, common practice was to have sailors in dress whites in the background of any major event. The ceremonies usually had nothing directly to do with the *Viperfish*; however, because our wide deck could accommodate several rows of photogenic enlisted men, we were often put through the paces.

Wherever we might be moored at the submarine base, the word regularly came down from above to sever our shore–power cables and prepare to move the *Viperfish* to a central pier location, in front of a cluster of chairs, for another ceremony. Those of us who either happened to be on duty that day or could not otherwise escape our impending fate were then ordered to put on dress whites, with the traditional black silk ties; balance sailor hats on our heads in the proper manner; and "lay topside" to relocate the boat and partake in a ceremony.

After moving the *Viperfish* across the base to the waters in front of the ceremony location, we formed several rows of clean–cut sailors standing at various degrees of attention in the relaxed manner that was classic for submarine sailors everywhere. We listened to long speeches about people we did not know, we watched boatswain's mates "pipe"* incoming officers into their

---

*The senior enlisted rating in the U.S. Navy is the boatswain's mate. Also called "bo's'n," the boatswain's mate has been in charge of the deck force of a ship since the days of sail. Setting the sails, heaving lines, and hoisting anchor required a coordinated team effort; the bo's'n's whistle signals coordinated the actions. When visitors to the sailing ships had to be hoisted aboard or lowered over the side, the bo's'n's pipe was used to order "Hoist away" or "Avast heaving." As time passed, piping a senior naval officer aboard became an established naval honor. The tradition remains strong, even in the nuclear era.

new command positions, and we stared at the seated spectators on the pier who stared back at us. At the conclusion of the ceremony, the new officers were in, the old officers were out, and most us returned to whatever we were doing before we were so rudely interrupted.

The arrival of Commander Harris was a different matter entirely. As our new captain, he was important to us because he would set the stage for the quality of our lives and play a major role in accomplishing the mission of the *Viperfish*. We had been told of his extensive background. He had served on board the USS *Trigger* (SS 564), *Sea Wolf* (SSN 575), and *Trinose* (SSN 606), and he was executive officer of the Polaris submarine, USS *Woodrow Wilson* (SSBN 624). We also knew that he had completed Admiral Rickover's "charm school" for the preparation of nuclear submarine commanding officers. There was a rumor that at the last moment, he had been diverted from going to sea on board the *Thresher* on her fatal voyage and that, as a result, he had recognized a higher calling. We had not yet seen the man, however; as far as we were concerned, Captain Harris was still an unknown factor.

When this change–of–command ceremony was announced, therefore, we paid close attention to the details. We moved the boat across the submarine base as usual and formed our rows in front of the same pier holding the same chairs. After listening to the same kind of speeches, we looked at the brow spanning from the pier to our boat and attentively watched Captain Harris come aboard.

He was a solid–looking man with a square jaw and bright blue eyes burning with the same kind of intensity that I had seen in Captain Gillon's. His manner appeared authoritative, yet reserved. In his brief conversation with us at the end of the ceremony, he spoke in a strong and deep voice. Although he gave away no secrets and revealed nothing about our future, he demonstrated a solid, intelligent style that reassured us. His final grade was still to be determined, but Captain Harris passed the crew's initial inspection.

His first action on board the *Viperfish* was to order replacement of all flickering or dim neon lights throughout the boat. Second, he established a higher level of cleanliness, underscoring the philosophy that morale and pride of serving on the *Viperfish* would improve. Third, he increased security for all of the secret documents on board. This action was the best clue that no word of our mission would ever leave the boat except under specific extraordinary circumstances, reserved only for information classified as "compartmentalized top secret." Because no information was provided to the crew, we assumed that everything relating to our mission was within this classification and continued to remain mystified about what lay ahead of us.

For the next several months, the men assigned to the Special Project team worked to refine the Fish and bring it up to operational capabilities. This required a series of trips from Pearl Harbor into the waters surrounding the Hawaiian Islands. Over and over again, our huge spool holding thousands of feet of cable was unreeled into the water. Far below us, the Fish was towed a few feet above the bottom of the ocean, and technical information acquired in this manner was evaluated and delivered back to the *Viperfish*.

Each trip lasted from a few days to several weeks, depending on where the *Viperfish* traveled and what activities were necessary. On some of the trips, we fired torpedoes and engaged in other actions that repeatedly went amazingly well. Our torpedoes were accurate, and our efficiency was high. As a result, the *Viperfish* earned the coveted Battle Efficiency "E" and the Fire Control Excellence Award for overall performance, reactor operations, torpedo firing capability, and operational capabilities. Captain Harris was off to a very good start.

In the traditional manner of Navy crews that earn their Battle Efficiency "E," we returned to port and proudly painted a large white "E" on the side of our sail. Although it occurred to many of us that the "E" was underwater and entirely out of sight most of the time, it provided us with a sense of camaraderie that was important to the morale of our crew and, hopefully, to our future success.

After each of our numerous patrols back and forth to the deeper waters east of Honolulu, Waikiki continued to beckon with the usual incentives to blow off steam. I became tired of paying the hefty fees for taxi rides between Pearl Harbor and Waikiki, so I finally purchased a blue 1955 Chevy from one of the many car lots in the Honolulu area. Although its metallic blue paint was scratched and slightly rusted, its front window had a small crack, and its carburetor leaked gasoline when the float repeatedly sank, it did have a sterling high-speed gearbox, definitely an outstanding feature of the car.

The first time I drove it off the base, Marc Birken challenged me on Kamehameha Highway as he revved his TR-3 engine and grinned like a fool. From his perspective, if it wasn't a sports car, it wasn't a *real* car. Meeting his challenge, I speed-shifted my new car up through the gears until the carburetor float sank and gasoline drowned the engine. Worried about fire and explosion from the reeking fumes, I quickly pulled over, ripped the carburetor apart, and listened to Marc contribute a long string of obscene and irreverent thoughts about my vehicle. I finally jammed a toothpick into the carburetor float hole to plug the leak forever, I hoped.

My qualifications efforts on the *Viperfish* continued, whether we were at sea or alongside the pier, as I struggled to learn every system on board the boat. Because I was finished with the nuclear qualifications work, the pressure in the engine room eased and my existence marginally improved. Also, because I was now standing watches at the reactor panel, I felt that I was finally carrying my own weight and contributing to the operations of the *Viperfish*. I visited Waikiki regularly, however, and surfed the waves at Sunset Beach on the island's north shore at every opportunity. Although I did not fully appreciate it at the time, being in the Navy and stationed in Hawaii probably constituted the best duty that any man could hope for.

On one of my trips to a dancing area in the Hilton Hawaiian Village, I asked a beautiful young lady to dance to the sweet Hawaiian music. She was a teacher, she said, at the Kamehameha Schools on the side of the hill behind Honolulu, and her name was Keiko. An hour later, she said she would certainly enjoy a midnight tour on a genuine nuclear submarine at Pearl Harbor. Her girlfriend and her date asked if they could come too, and soon all four of us piled into my Chevy for the run up to the submarine base.

After a few scans through the control-room periscope to look at the distant lights of Pearl City and a stroll through the remainder of the *Viperfish*'s control center, we took another tour of Makaha Beach under the moonlight at two o'clock in the morning. After that remarkable evening, Keiko and I dated every night that I was in port. We found ourselves aware of an emerging intensity and a new fulfillment that strongly attracted us to each other. As we spent more time together, I found it increasingly difficult to break away from the sweet time on liberty with her, to drive back to Pearl Harbor, and to climb down the engine-room hatch as the *Viperfish* prepared to go to sea.

Keiko flew back to Los Angeles to continue working on her master's degree at the University of Southern California, while her girlfriend stayed behind and married the young man she had met that night. That was when Keiko informed her parents, both working full time to finance her USC tuition, about the sailor in Hawaii who had asked for her hand in marriage.

"And, you told him?" her father asked, his voice hardening, his mind struggling to remain rational.

"I told him, 'yes,'" Keiko answered, bracing herself.

"And, this man is an officer in the United States Navy?" His voice rose an octave.

"Well, sort of. He works in the engine room of..."

"Then, he has completed college?"

"Well, he *does* have some college credits, before he joined the Navy. At least, I think he finished part of the first year. He is planning on going back to school after he's out of the Navy."

"Keiko!" Her father's voice assumed a rigid quality and sounded like it always did when there was to be no further discussion.

"Yes?"

"I think you should wait."

"Dad," she said patiently and without hesitation, "when I finish my master's program next year, we are going to get married."

Her mother stopped knitting. After a moment of silence, she finally provided the maternal viewpoint, "I'm sure this boy is a fine young man."

Keiko continued her education at USC, and her parents scheduled an engagement dinner in Southern California.

For the next two months, the *Viperfish* sat anchored two miles off the northwest coast of Maui, near the small town of Lahaina. The waters were stunningly clear. Looking straight down from the edge of the deck, we could see details in the sand at the bottom of the ocean. We were going to finish testing the Fish, Captain Harris told us. This would include its electronic capabilities, to be evaluated in shallow waters, and the clear water off Maui was perfect.

Anchored within viewing distance of Lahaina, our large black submarine was a strange sight. Many of the tourists showed considerable curiosity about our boat. Various sailboats and catamarans set out from the Lahaina harbor to encircle us. People took pictures and waved, called "Aloha!" and exchanged pleasantries with us as we wandered around in dungarees on the topside deck. For those of us not actively involved with testing the Fish, the days were filled with long watches in front of our nuclear control panels in the engine room. The civilians worked vigorously with the complex Fish in the hangar compartment and created a number of enhancements that would allow the future accumulation of data from far below the surface of the ocean.

Much of the Special Project testing was done at night in order to simulate the great depths of the dark ocean. The brilliant lighting system of the Fish created flashing distractions for cars moving along the Honoapiilani Highway. We received reports from Lahaina that the bright strobe flashes, lighting up the ocean at odd times throughout the night, contributed to a couple of automobile crashes, although we were never able to confirm the details.

Except for the occasional bombs exploding on the Navy's Kahoolawe Island bombing range twenty miles across the Auau Channel, most of us felt that we had entered the ultimate paradise of submarine duty. We enjoyed barbecues on the topside deck as we watched smiling bikini–clad beauties passing by on sailboats. We also played on rubber rafts around the *Viperfish* and dove into the ocean, from time to time, to look at the colorful fish.

When the bombing became intense, as it sometimes did, Paul Mathews or whoever was on duty in the control room announced over the loudspeakers, "Navy jets closing off starboard bow!" Those of us not on watch scrambled out of the hatches to watch the high–speed Navy fighters streaking across the ocean, pointing directly at us, and presumably lining up the *Viperfish* as a target. After screaming over the top of our boat, the aircraft fired their afterburners and headed directly up the side of the nearly 6,000–foot peak of Maui's Puu Ku Kui mountain behind Lahaina. Finally, they flew straight up into the sky and disappeared from sight. Although the Vietnam War seemed a million miles away as we floated on those peaceful Hawaiian waters, we suspected that many of the pilots crossing over our boat were en route to Southeast Asia. A glance at any daily newspaper told us that many of them would not return.

When I wasn't staring at the meters on the reactor control panel or watching strafing runs on the *Viperfish*, I continued with my qualifications activities. I was moving progressively closer to learning everything I could about our submarine. The entire process seemed endless, but the list of systems that I still had to learn was getting shorter and the precious dolphins began to appear attainable. The biggest activity of the *Viperfish*, the Special Project with its team of engineers, was not on my list. We still had been told virtually nothing about our secret Fish and its miles of cables. Because we did not have a "need to know" for performance of our duties, silence on the subject was the order of the day.

Another thirty or forty jets completed their runs on the *Viperfish* during the following month. We watched every one of them. The Fish strobe light illuminated most of the undersea life near the western coast of Maui, and we scanned and photographed every-thing within sight. After enough experience with the Fish had been accumulated to satisfy Captain Harris and the hangar scien-tists, we pulled everything related to the Special Project inside the *Viperfish* and returned to Pearl Harbor.

On a beautiful Monday morning several weeks later, Captain Harris ordered ten of us to report to the topside deck in our dress whites to receive our coveted silver dolphins. It had taken more than a year for me to master each system that filled the compart-ments of the *Viperfish*, and this award signified an end to that long struggle. I now belonged to the select club of those who are deemed "qualified in submarines."

Captain Harris lined up the ten of us in front of the rest of the crew. He said some words about the importance of our accom-plishments and his personal appreciation for an increase in the number of men qualified on the *Viperfish*. After pinning the dol-phins on our spotless uniforms, he posed with us for the official photograph documenting the event and then quickly moved from the area as we came under immediate attack by the rest of the qualified crew of the *Viperfish*.

Led by Paul Mathews and Randy Nicholson, they cut off our escape and went after each of us with great enthusiasm. We scat-tered across the deck. I fought valiantly, but several of the nukes caught me scrambling up the side of the bat-cave hump. Holding my arms and legs, they dragged me to the edge of the *Viperfish* deck to begin swinging me for the launch overboard.

"Wait!" I yelled. "Let me save my wallet!"

"To hell with your wallet!" they hollered back in unison, all of them grinning with delight.

They swung me higher and higher and the launch became imminent.

"Let me save my shoes! I just polished my shoes this morning."

"To hell with your shoes!"

"I have money in my wallet!" I was getting desperate.

The swinging immediately stopped.

"He has money in his wallet," Nicholson repeated.

"Grab his wallet, protect his money!" somebody else said.

Groping hands whipped out my wallet, while a kindly benefactor ripped off my shoes. Around me, I could hear the sounds of other men yelling, followed by the noise of numerous bodies hitting the ocean. I grabbed the arm of one of my tormentors in the hope of taking him with me, but my grip was immediately broken. Vicelike claws encircled my arms and legs, and the swinging began again.

On the count of three, the men launched me far out into the waters of Pearl Harbor. Spiraling around and around, I somersaulted through the air. My head hit the water first, my sailor hat floating behind me like a strange white Frisbee and my neatly pressed uniform ruined forever. I bubbled back up to the surface and lifted my head out of the water to see the crew watching the show from the edge of the *Viperfish*'s deck. I grabbed my hat before it sank out of sight and swam back with the others to the boat, where several men helped us onto the deck. Standing in front of the crew and dripping salt water from my oil-stained uniform, I enthusiastically shook everybody's hand and felt the crew's camaraderie and acceptance.

Throwing a newly qualified man overboard, a tradition as old as the dolphins, is an important part of the Submarine Service. In a perverse manner, it signifies the respect from men who, in the years ahead, would depend on the new man's skills when machinery failed and his actions could determine the fate of the crew.

I have been told of occasions when submarine crews refused to throw newly qualified men overboard, although I never did see this occur while I was on board the *Viperfish*. That action is the most visible rejection that a potential submariner can receive. It is reserved for the rare man who is felt to be unworthy of the dolphins, even though he received all of the necessary signatures on his qualifications card. The rest of the crew members do not consider him to be a *shipmate,* and their rejection can be compared to an unseen scarlet letter. The usual result is that the man finally transfers off the boat.

I called my parents that night to tell them about achieving my dolphins and the unusual ceremony to mark the event. To my surprise, they spoke in somber tones as they congratulated me. Then, they informed me about disruptions among the family in California that were acting to fragment it. The cause was the Vietnam War, they said, and the issue was creating a turmoil that was distressing everyone. My sister's husband, Brad, a man who had served in the Navy many years before and who had encouraged me to join the service, had now become an antiwar activist. He was polarized on the subject, my parents said, and he could not even talk about Vietnam without becoming enraged. They encouraged me not to mention the war if I talked to him in the future. My little brother, Gerry, they continued, was finishing high school and had no interest in joining the Navy or becoming a part of any military service.

"But South Vietnam is depending on us!" I said, feeling an anger that surprised me. "We promised them, we can't just back out now!"

"Just don't bring up the subject around Brad," my father said. "You're in the service and you represent the war in a lot of their minds, especially those who are protesting. Don't bring up the subject, and don't try to discuss it if Brad brings it up."

"The protesters are all smoking pot, or bananas, or whatever they can find! I didn't start the war–"

"I know that, but it doesn't matter."

"It doesn't matter? It's the truth!"

"It's hard to tell where the truth is, these days. The whole damn country seems to be falling apart. There's a lot of men dying in Vietnam–"

"And we can't let them die in vain! Haven't you ever heard of the domino theory?"

I was the hawk, my Mom and Dad were neutral, my sister's husband would tear me apart if I brought up the subject, and my brother considered military service to be undesirable. I thanked them for bringing me up to date about my family and hung up, feeling a sense of hopelessness about the entire subject. Walking back to the *Viperfish*, I wondered again about our mission, and I worried about how much longer the Vietnam War would last.

▲
Four shipmates at sea
on board the *Viperfish*.

The *Viperfish* firing a Regulus I missile during surfaced testing operations, early 1960s.
▼

The *Viperfish* during surfaced operations in the Pacific Ocean, 1967. Note the increased height of her sail and the presence of a bow thruster motor on the forward deck.

▼

▲

The *Viperfish*, departing Pearl Harbor and the
island of Oahu, as she prepares to submerge
on her first patrol.

The *Viperfish* alongside the pier at the Pearl Harbor Submarine Base during change–of–command ceremony.
▼

▲
Newly qualified submariners, on the deck of the *Viperfish*,
shortly after receiving their dolphins from the captain.
The author is standing, far left.

▲

The off-watch crew of the *Viperfish*, as she passes
San Francisco's Golden Gate Bridge.

◀ Dolphin ceremony on the deck of the *Viperfish*. The captain
awards dolphins to the author. At the far left is the "bat cave"
door, and standing nearby are several qualified crew members
waiting to initiate the traditional overboard ceremony.

▲
The *Viperfish*, crossing
San Francisco Bay.

Torpedo recovery activities, at sea ▶
near the island of Maui.

▲
Small–arms target practice, at sea in the mid–Pacific.

▲
The author in steam suit, accompanied by
the *Viperfish*'s corpsman, in the tunnel over the
nuclear reactor compartment.

▲
The nuclear–trained men practicing a
steam leak drill in the *Viperfish* tunnel.

▲

The *Viperfish*, surfaced off the coast of Maui, during testing of the Fish. The "bat cave" door, leading to the hangar space below, is open, and several crewmen are on the deck.

MINOR FAILURES, MAJOR LOSSES

IN CALIFORNIA, THE HALLUCINOGENIC EFFECT of smoking dried banana peels was found to produce a mild "trip," and students at the University of California at Berkeley held mass banana "smokeouts." As interest in another hallucinogenic drug, lysergic acid diethylamide (LSD), increased across the country, scientists reported the first evidence of drug–induced chromosomal changes suspected to cause mental retardation in the children of pregnant women who used LSD. After failing to register as a narcotics violator, Dr. Timothy Leary, former Harvard University professor and founder of the LSD religious cult, was arrested by U.S. Customs officials while promoting his beliefs on the use of LSD. New York City's Bellevue Hospital reported the admission of more than 130 LSD users, many suffering from profound terror, uncontrolled violence, and attempted homicide or suicide. A member of California's Neuropsychiatric Institute informed the American College Health Association in Washington, D.C., that 30 percent of the students in certain high schools had become established users of LSD.

In the Soviet Union, in spite of the numerous problems of radiation, detection, and maintenance of operational capability, the eventual success of the Echo II SSGN testing program established the guided missile submarine in the position of a third order of battle (behind the ballistic missile SSBN Hotel class and the converted Golf and Zulu ballistic missile submarines). When the testing was concluded and the vessels were finally ready for duty, the Soviet crews prepared for prolonged voyages and the fulfillment of their missions in the Pacific Ocean.

▼

KEIKO FLEW BACK for a few days on Oahu before the *Viperfish* left for sea to begin the final deep-sea testing of the Fish and the Special Project system. Her father had reluctantly agreed to our marriage, scheduled for June 1968, and she told me of the disruptions on the campus at USC caused by the antiwar protesters, who were now burning their draft cards and yelling, "Hell no, we won't go!"

The two of us had some quiet time together, and Keiko came to the pier with the relatives of the crew to watch us leave for our prolonged patrol. I was already depressed about our separation. For Keiko to watch me go, in many ways, intensified the ordeal of leaving her.

We cleared the Pearl Harbor channel, dropped deep below the surface, and proceeded to the waters off the west coast of the island of Hawaii. The men in the hangar space, working vigorously to prepare our system for its test, checked the tiny high-strength wires welded together to form the cable, measured various test signals provided by the Fish, and tried to make everything work properly. We slowed to all ahead one-third at a depth of three hundred feet and lowered the Fish toward the bottom, nearly fifteen thousand feet below.

We assumed the usual condition of seemingly motionless existence, our little world of men and machinery moving back and forth over the various peaks, valleys, and plateaus at the bottom of the ocean as we gathered data from the Fish. After a week of testing the system, we rolled the cable back onto the spool just before the sonar operator reported that his BQS–4 sonar system had detected a nearby surface craft.

"Hammerclaw! Hammerclaw!" the underwater telephone voice from the ship blasted into the control center. This was the call sign designated for the *Viperfish.*

Captain Harris grabbed the microphone near the control center and called back a response. He informed the ship that the submarine code–named Hammerclaw was, in fact, nearby. We eased up to periscope depth; the captain and Lt. Comdr. Duane Ryack, the executive officer (XO), raised the two periscopes, and we waited for the beginning of the choreographed action, created weeks in advance of our rendezvous.

The plan was quite simple. The surface ship would bring a target with a characteristic shape into our vicinity and prepare to drop it to the bottom near the island of Hawaii. Because the shape could give away the nature of our future mission, it was classified top secret and enclosed in a huge sealed box on the deck of the vessel. A crane on the ship would lower the box into the water. When the bottom of the box was pulled away, the mystery object would disappear into the depths before the ship's crew had a chance to see it. We would search the bottom of the ocean with our Fish after the ship departed the area and, hopefully, identify the object's location and appearance.

Perhaps the plan was too simple. We continued to cruise slowly at a depth of sixty–five feet, as Captain Harris and the XO watched the ship through our periscopes and called out her every move to us.

"They have raised the box off the side of the ship and it is now being lowered to the water," Captain Harris called. He clicked the periscope to higher power and narrowed his eyes. "The box is now in the water, the release is imminent."

A few moments passed, and Commander Ryack called out from the port periscope, "They have released the object and they are lifting the box off the water."

One of the officers suddenly exclaimed, "Oh, my God!" as the other shouted, "I cannot believe this...the target is floating."

They stared at each other as a voice from the ship's radiotelephone boomed into our control center.

"Now, Hammerclaw, Hammerclaw! There will be a delay in the dropping of the target. Repeat, delay."

The problem was the density of the object. Whoever had prepared it had neglected to determine whether the density of the thing was greater than the density of the ocean water it was to displace. Unfortunately for the secrecy of the entire operation, the object was too light to sink. The shape that nobody was supposed to see was floating at the side of the ship while the crane operators, deckhands, and everybody else stared at it.

After the thing had been fully observed by everyone on the ship, her crew hauled it back to the deck and set about furiously wrapping it with heavy chains and even a couple of anchors for added weight. When the object was finally covered with enough junk to sink a battleship, they shoved the entire mess overboard and it immediately sank out of sight. We heard a sad "Farewell to Hammerclaw" over our underwater telephone as the ship turned away and prepared to take on board a naval intelligence team, scrambled to the area on an intercept vessel to address the massive breach of security. The word later filtered down to us that every man on the ship was interrogated in an intensive debriefing process during the Navy's struggle to negate security leaks that could compromise our mission.

We lowered the Fish thousands of feet out of the *Viperfish* and began searching the bottom again. Locked in our motionless world once again, we stood watches, ate our meals, watched movies, occasionally showered, and wondered what the shape could be.

Several of the crew and I were sitting in the dining area when photographer Robbie Teague walked in with a handful of 8 × 10 glossy black-and-white photos and an excited but secretive expression on his face. All of us liked Robbie; he was a small fellow with a quiet and pleasant manner. He conscientiously worked to generate the highest-quality pictures that our equipment could produce.

"What do you have there, Robbie?" Sandy Gallivan asked, looking at the photographs.

"Interesting pictures?" I chimed in.

"Dirty pictures from Tijuana?" Birken asked, with raised eyebrows and a grin.

Robbie laid the pictures on the table and we all gathered around.

"We have found our target!" he said, his voice charged with excitement. "The guys in the hangar are pretty excited."

As we looked at the pictures, Gallivan asked the obvious question.

"These are great pictures, Robbie, but where's the target?"

Robbie looked surprised and then offended. "It's right there!" He pointed at the corner of the nearest picture. "It's right next to the anchor and chain you can see here in the corner!"

"All I see is an anchor and chain," I said.

"And mud." Birken added.

Robbie straightened his short frame and tried to look indignant.

"You know we can't show you the actual target, the skipper won't allow it. It's top secret!" he said. "But, we found it!"

"Great!" Birken said as he turned to leave the area. "I'm going to hit the rack."

"Robbie, what are we looking for?" I asked.

He pointed at his pictures again. "The shape, the target, the thing we just—"

"Not that, Robbie, what is the *real* thing? What are we getting ready for?"

He studied Marc and me for a moment, and finally answered, "Everything is so goddamn secret that even I don't know what we're doing. And I'm part of the Special Project team. Okay, I know the shape, but I don't think this thing is the real target. I think our real target, whatever it is that we are going to be looking for out there, has yet to be defined."

He glanced around us, ensuring that the room was empty, and his voice dropped to a whisper. "Even the civilians in the hangar don't know, if you can believe that. Even the officers in the wardroom don't know. The captain and the XO are the only ones who have a clue and sometimes I wonder if even they know the whole story. My guess is that this is a project in evolution."

The next day, we lost the Fish. Two days later, we lost our nuclear reactor.

The problem with the Fish was the cable and its assembly design, which brought together many strands of wire. Each wire was constructed with extraordinary tensile strength and flexibility to withstand the many flexings associated with wrapping it around the spool, but when two strands were welded together, a weak spot was generated. As the long cable was rolled around the spool, some of the strands broke, which created a snarl of wire that prevented us from pulling the Fish all the way back into the boat.

Having an immovable long cable, extending from our belly, attached to an extremely sensitive and expensive device jammed with electronics was a disaster for the testing program. The civilians and Special Project officers grappled with the dilemma but told the rest of us nothing. Finally, they removed the cable from its attachment point on the spool, and the entire assembly, including the Fish, was dropped to the ocean floor thousands of feet below the *Viperfish*.

Although there were no announcements to the rest of us, the glum demeanor of those associated with the Fish left no doubt as to the outcome of their efforts. The *Viperfish* had been budgeted for a total of five Fish, and we had carried two; the $55 million allowance for our backup Fish suddenly appeared to be money well spent. We turned and headed in the direction of Pearl Harbor.

On watch two days later, I was sitting in front of the reactor control panel as we dropped down about two hundred and fifty feet and steamed along at full power. I logged in the initial set of reactor readings and then sat back in my chair to scan the meters showing everything of significance about our nuclear plant.

Suddenly, the shrieking noise of multiple reactor alarms blasted me from my seat. As I always did when the reactor control panel turned into a maze of flashing red lights, I stood up, kicked over the coffeepot near my foot, and started hitting various switches across the panel. One of the nuclear machinist mates, Billy Elstner, sitting below us in his tight corner of the lower-level engine room, knew instantly from the rain of coffee on his head that a major problem was developing in the maneuvering room.

"The reactor is shut down!" I hollered. Searching the flashing red lights across the panel for any clue as to what had happened, I felt certain that this was another damnable drill. Admiral Rickover's crew of "NR boys" from the Naval Reactor Division in Washington was scheduled to test our knowledge after we returned to Pearl Harbor, and I figured Captain Harris was throwing another nuclear test our way to prepare us.

After announcing the shutdown to the control center, Lt. John Pintard, engineering officer of the watch, yelled from his position behind me, "What is the cause of the shutdown?"

"No indication, sir!" I hollered back, searching for any abnormalities. "Initiating emergency reactor start-up!"

"Very well!" Pintard said, watching the start-up process begin.

I began flipping switches to bring the reactor back up to power. Donald Svedlow, sitting next to me, raced his hands back and forth across his electrical panel and opened circuit breakers throughout the engine room as the steam pressure feeding his turbogenerators began to drop.

"Rig ship for reduced power!" crackled out of the ship's loudspeakers. The crew ran around the boat and turned off power-consuming equipment to conserve energy. As the air conditioner compressors were de-energized and the cool air in the ventilation pipes became humid and warm, the engine room began to heat up.

The reactor fission level finally started to increase as I continued the effort to restart the plant. Meanwhile, everybody scouted around the compartment and searched the engine-room electronic systems for any clue as to why the shutdown happened. Just as I brought the reactor power back into heat–producing capability again, Rossi showed up in the maneuvering room.

"What shut us down?" Pintard asked.

"No clue, sir," Rossi said. "The instrumentation showed no abnormality. Nothing in the–"

He was interrupted by another blast of alarms from my panel. The reactor had shut down again.

"Reactor shutdown, sir!" I hollered to the EOOW, as I kicked the empty coffeepot.

I immediately initiated the emergency start–up operation, while the chief of the boat from the control center announced over the loudspeakers, "Surface! Surface! Surface!"

"What the hell is going on?" Rossi exclaimed, as he spun around and left the maneuvering room to search our electronic systems for some indication of why we kept shutting down.

Our engine–room loudspeakers carried Captain Harris's voice: "This is not a drill! Repeat, this is not a drill!"

The *Viperfish*, angling steeply upward as we thundered to the surface, finally broke through and immediately began to roll heavily in the turbulent ocean. The temperature in the engine room quickly climbed to more than 100 degrees, and our uniforms became drenched in sweat.

"Starting up, again, sir!" I called out, as I flipped more switches and turned the levers controlling the reactor.

"Moving to battery power, sir!" Svedlow called out as he slammed open more circuit breakers throughout the engine room.

As the fission level began to climb, we heard Rossi hollering from the passageway that nothing was wrong, that all instruments showed normal reactor operations.

The alarms suddenly fired again, with red lights pulsating all over the panel.

"We're down again, sir!" I yelled.

"What the hell is this?" Pintard roared, his eyes darting back and forth from my panel to Svedlow's panel in search of clues.

Before I could even think about trying to start the reactor again, numerous changes within the pressurized-water reactor system showed that I was rapidly losing all control of the reactor.

"She's shutting down more, sir!" I called out.

"Goddamnit, she's shutting all the way down!" Pintard hollered.

I grabbed my levers and tried to stop the accelerating shutdown. I hollered "Mr. Pintard!" and, standing in front of the panel, pointed speechless at the rapidly changing indicators. At that moment, I clearly had no control of the systems that determine the reactor fission levels.

Although I had once thought I would never be required to take the next action, I reached over to the panel and grabbed the large steel protective guard enclosing the biggest switch on the board.

"Permission to SCRAM the plant, sir!" I yelled as loudly as possible, and Pintard immediately hollered back, "SCRAM the goddamn plant!"

I clutched the black switch under the guard. With a quick flip of my wrist, I snapped the switch to the right, which caused the circuits controlling the power levels of the nuclear reactor to initiate a total and complete emergency shutdown.

"The plant is scrammed and we are totally shut down, sir!"

"Very well, Dunham," Pintard answered, grabbing his engine room microphone. "Now, the reactor is scrammed, the reactor is scrammed!" he announced.

For the next ten hours, we rolled around on the surface, the hangar containing the remnants of our lost Fish system and the engine room holding the broken electronics that controlled our reactor. The *Viperfish* seemed to be falling apart in spite of our best efforts to make everything work properly.

Rossi and the other men in the Reactor Control Division tore through the circuit drawers with voltmeters and flashlights. They dripped sweat into the circuits and pored over pages of schematics as they tried to find the source of the problem. Most of this time, Captain Harris sat on the steps of the steaming upper-level engine room and watched his men struggling to find out why the *Viperfish* no longer had a functioning nuclear reactor.

After several hours of testing and intense thinking, Rossi finally found the problem. A diode, a tiny piece of electronic equipment, worth about forty-nine cents in any Radio Shack store, had burned out. As its internal electron-controlling capability failed, intermittently at first and finally permanently, the cascade of erroneous electronic messages caused the shutdown of circuits in a manner that left no clue. This flawed diode was the sole reason for the strange reactor shutdowns that had brought us to the surface.

Rossi tore the offending piece of electronic junk out of its soldered connection and replaced it with a new one. A half hour later, the reactor worked perfectly. The prolonged start-up went smoothly, no red lights flashed, no alarms blared, and the machinist mates below the maneuvering room experienced no further dousing of coffee. The turbines were soon screaming, and we were churning up the Pacific. The captain took the *Viperfish* down to two hundred feet. The air-conditioning systems were turned on, and cool air blew once again. We finished our trip back to Pearl without further problems.

Keiko had returned to Los Angeles to continue with her studies, so nobody was waiting on the pier for me. I had no time to feel lonely, however, because another group of visitors, the "NR boys from Admiral Rickover," awaited all of us who worked in the nuclear field. We were scheduled to take a Nuclear Reactor (NR) Board examination soon after our return, a regular occurrence on all nuclear submarines of the U.S. Navy. The directive for the examination came from the man in charge of naval nuclear propulsion operations, the man we called the Great White Father.

Admiral Rickover was widely regarded as the "Father of the Nuclear Navy." Most of us, however, considered him less impressive than did the general public. We were in awe of the man, not so much because of his many accomplishments during the early development of the nuclear Navy but as a result of the raw fear that he engendered in the men working in this field. Our engineering officers often related stories of their interviews with Rickover. They said that he threw chairs across the room, screamed orders not to talk when an airplane was flying overhead, seated the interviewees in unstable chairs, and exhibited enough strange actions to fill a book. Each engineering officer had a different set of stories to tell–the *Viperfish's* file of interview stories was voluminous. Although they were a source of entertainment during our long patrols, the stories conveyed to us a sense of instability. Further, many of the men on board the *Viperfish* felt that Rickover had a disturbing tendency to destroy brilliant naval careers without remorse.

His defenders struggled to justify this seemingly irrational behavior as the admiral's way of prevailing against dissenting opinions, as well as a means of creating stress in order to test the worth of prospective engineers and commanding officers. Although there might have been some element of truth here, we felt that other methods would have been more effective and less destructive to the careers of men who suffered at his hands. When the admiral's substantial political power base was unable to prevent Secretary of the Navy John Lehman from retiring him in the early 1980s, a large number of men whose naval careers had been damaged or terminated felt some measure of satisfaction that his reign was finally over.

For those of us responsible for the *Viperfish's* nuclear propulsion system, however, there was the immediate need to pass Admiral Rickover's NR examination. The men sent by Rickover were lean, crisp, and very bright, and I knew that they would ask every conceivable detailed question about our operation of the nuclear plant. There would be no sliding by; as Bruce Rossi warned us, we should answer their questions briskly and present an appearance of having substantial knowledge.

The three examiners took us, one at a time, into a small conference room in a quiet corner of the submarine base. I was called first and seated on the far side of a large wooden table holding a stack of the *Viperfish*'s reactor plant manuals, while the examiners stared at me in a manner that stimulated raw fear.

"You are Petty Officer Second Class Roger C. Dunham, right?" the leanest and most intense of them finally asked after an indeterminate period of time.

"Yes, sir," I answered, bracing myself for the first question.

"You are one of the *Viperfish*'s nuclear reactor operators, right?"

"Yes, sir."

The officer folded his hands on the table in front of him and stared at me again.

"Good," he said, his face showing a glint of eagerness as he moved in for the kill. "Tell us what your immediate action would be if the reactor's electronic shutdown banks generated an emergency condition from the activation of the CR–389 circuit, causing a sudden loss of reactor power."

I stared at the man, his words tumbling through my brain, while I tried to remember anything on the *Viperfish* that resembled a CR circuit. Taking a deep breath, I considered a variety of responses and finally said, "Sir, would you please repeat the question?"

The man glanced at his NR colleagues and stared back at me as though I were the most stupid human being he had ever seen.

"I *said*, tell us what your immediate action would be if the reactor's electronic shutdown banks generated an emergency condition from the activation of the CR–389 circuit, causing sudden loss of power. Can you do that for us?"

Rivers of sweat began to flow from my armpits as I realized I didn't have a clue as to what he was talking about. I had never even heard of a CR circuit or anything like it. I had been spending most of the past six months studying shutdowns, dreaming shutdowns, experiencing shutdowns, and his question rang no bells. Three pairs of eyes glared at me from across the table.

"I believe, sir," I said, struggling to sound intelligent, "that the CR–389 circuit is an anomalous system installed since I last reviewed the reactor plant manuals, and whatever its intended action may have been at the time of its installation, it is not now operational on the *Viperfish*."

If my answer was wrong, I was dead. The *Viperfish* would be zapped of its newest reactor operator. I would be sent to Adak, Alaska, where the frozen tundra and the Rat Islands accumulated destroyed careers, and Keiko and I would freeze to death. It did not enter my mind that these men might not know what they were talking about—they were officers, they were trained in nuclear engineering, and they were sent by the Great White Father. They designed nuclear plants and invented complex questions based on their detailed knowledge.

They had to know the answers.

None of these considerations made CR circuits any more apparent to me. As I watched them confer, I hoped that they would turn in my direction and say that they had "the right circuit but, sorry, Petty Officer Dunham, the wrong name." One of them casually flipped open one of the reactor plant manuals and the other two studied the pages before them in silence. They conferred again, slapped the book shut, and then looked at me.

"Petty Officer Dunham, would you please describe the emergency reactor shutdown system on the USS *Viperfish?*"

CR circuits no longer on the table, I took off like somebody had ignited my afterburners. I told them about the circuits, I described what would happen inside the reactor as the result of different signals, I told them about forty–nine–cent diodes that could jeopardize the mission of a multimillion dollar submarine, and I provided heaping servings of fission flux talk that brought smiles to their faces.

When I finished, I mentioned that I had not heard of the CR–389 circuit but I would be happy to learn everything about it, if they would like to share the information with me.

The lean one, the most intense one, showed just a trace of uncertainty as he asked, "Your nuclear plant is an S5W reactor, right?"

Stunned, I stared back at him. Almost all of the submarines in the U.S. fleet carried the S5W reactor. British submarines carried it, and our government had even offered the French an S5W reactor.

But the *Viperfish* was different.

"Actually, sir," I said politely, "we have the S3W plant on the *Viperfish*. It is a weird system, and it has some technology that is a little out of date, but it does do the job."

The interview came to a rapid close a few minutes later, following a couple of final cursory questions. I thanked them and left. They remained in the room with our reactor plant manuals as they studied and puzzled over what the *Viperfish* was all about, including its strange S3W reactor. We were later told that we did well on the exam, and Admiral Rickover indicated to Captain Harris that his crew of nuclear-trained men were a credit to his submarine. The other men and I speculated over cold brews at Fort DeRussy later that night what the response of the Great White Father would be if we were to send the Pentagon a letter suggesting that his NR boys also undergo a board exam.

We loaded a new Fish, jammed with the same electronics as the one lying somewhere on the bottom of the Pacific, and headed back to sea for a final series of tests. All of us felt certain that, somewhere in the back rooms of the Pentagon, a decision had been made not to try to find our lost Fish. There would have been no way to recover it, and there was little value in knowing where the device, with its miles of cable, had come to rest.

When we flooded one week later, the depth of the ocean was about three times the crush depth of the *Viperfish*.

The flooding resulted from yet another broken system, this one located at the top of the snorkel mast. Because our submarine was without fresh air for prolonged periods of time, the air was regularly contaminated by smoke from cigarettes, pipes, and cigars, as well as gases from record-setting belches and fumes from the sanitary tanks and other significant sources. All of this mandated an occasional cleansing of the atmosphere. Beyond surfacing and pumping in fresh air from our open hatches, the only other way to accomplish this was to raise a pipe, called the snorkel mast, above the ocean surface and suck in fresh air with a huge air pump. This air then circulated throughout the boat, a freshening process that seemed to clear our minds and improve morale.

Because ocean waves vary in height, a valve-closure system was introduced on the USS *Darter* (SS 576) in 1957 to shut the opening to the intake pipe if water from a wave flowed over the snorkel. The system worked well most of the time, although we regularly experienced fluctuations in eardrum pressure whenever the valve shut and the air pump created a vacuum. We became proficient at grabbing our noses and blowing to equalize the pressure in our inner ears when this occurred. Anybody failing to take this action was at risk of a ruptured eardrum.

I was off watch and sound asleep in my rack when the snorkel system failed. We were submerged at periscope depth, with the top of our snorkel mast stuck out of the ocean as the pump circulated air through the vents. A wave lifted over the top of the snorkel and broke off a metallic indicator device at the top of the valve just before the valve slammed shut. The broken piece of metal was immediately wedged inside the seat of the valve, which resulted in an opening that allowed seawater to be sucked rapidly into the *Viperfish*. As the weight of the water (more than two thousand pounds in the main induction pipe alone) added to the weight of the boat, we immediately dropped farther under the surface and continued to suck in more seawater, which, of course, made us heavier and dropped us even deeper.

The first indication that I had of a problem was the blast of cold ocean water spraying against the right side of my head and covering my pillow, mattress, and blanket. My eyes flew open. Bolting upright, I smashed my head into the underside of the rack above me and heard Chief Mathews announce, "Surface, surface, surface!" over the boat's loudspeaker system. As I leaped out of my rack, the bow began pointing steeply upward and I could hear the roaring noise from the blowing of our ballast tanks.

Captain Harris was urgently awakened by Commander Ryack, who tapped him on the shoulder.

"Captain," Ryack said, "we're having a bit of a problem in the control room." As the captain swung his feet to the deck and stood up, he noticed that he was ankle deep in water.

We quickly surfaced. As the top of the snorkel cleared the surface of the ocean, water stopped pouring out of our ventilation vents. The ballast control operator's quick corrective action of turning off the main induction pump after seeing it fill with water (visualized through a tiny window called the bulls-eye, designed for this purpose) probably saved the *Viperfish* from sinking. At the very least, he saved a prolonged period of shipyard repairs.

So, we had another cleanup operation, this one involving the washing and drying of electronic equipment that, unfortunately, was lying in the vicinity of the ventilation vents. The radiomen were especially upset by the damage to their delicate receivers, several of which received considerable saltwater contamination.

I pulled out my pillow and blankets to air dry them, and several other men repaired damage to personal items, such as books and pictures, stored in their racks. I tucked clean sheets around my mattress and then turned my attention to the battery well under the crew's berthing passageway. I was aware of saltwater and electrochemical conversions, the patterns of chlorine gas generation, and the deadly effects of the gas on living tissue. As I walked toward the hole leading to the battery, I noted that, fortunately, the area was dry in spite of the flooding, but I wondered about the consequences of a few thousand gallons of seawater pouring into the battery well should a more substantial event occur. I also wondered how quickly 120 men could escape a submarine filling with chlorine gas.

The failures of machinery on the *Viperfish* affected our psyches far more than our substance. Although Captain Harris's calm style of leadership rallied us to have faith in our future, we did not accomplish this without some collective soul searching. The unpredictable, random nature of the failures and the potentials for disaster from such tiny malfunctions created special concerns. If a couple of small wires on a cable could cost us weeks of work and the loss of a Fish worth millions of dollars, if a tiny diode could shut down a powerful nuclear reactor and stop a submarine, and if an indicator device no bigger than a finger could cause a serious flood within the internal spaces of the *Viperfish*, what would happen if something of real significance went wrong?

Again and again, it came down to the spirit, the training, and the quality of the crew that made the difference. Machinery fails, and anything as complex as an operational nuclear submarine can have many failures. When wires break, diodes burn out, and water floods into the boat, the reactions of the crew, borne by training and spirit, determine the outcome. As we completed the final preparations for our secret mission, it was my hope that the remarkable quality of the *Viperfish* crew would allow us to prevail during the months ahead, no matter what dangers awaited us beneath the sea.

THE DOMAIN OF THE
GOLDEN DRAGON

THE FIRST SIX MONTHS of 1968 brought armed conflict and disaster to ships and submarines around the world. In January, the
Soviet Union protested the dropping of eight time-bombs by
"American jets" on the Soviet freighter *Pereslavl-Zalessky* in
Haiphong Harbor, North Vietnam, that reportedly damaged the
ship's engine room. Within a day of this event, bombs from U.S.
military planes struck the Chinese Communist ship *Hongqi-158* in
the North Vietnamese port of Cam Pha. Several crewmen were
wounded, and the vessel was seriously damaged.

On January 23, North Korean naval vessels attacked the spy
ship USS *Pueblo* in international waters. Although the ship transmitted numerous radio calls for help during the 2½-hour attack,
U.S. naval forces, located far to the south, were unable to provide
assistance. An enlisted man was killed during the initial attack, as
the commanding officer, Comdr. Lloyd M. Bucher, frantically
struggled to clarify international law relating to "rights of
retrieval" of the *Pueblo*'s top secret equipment from the ocean floor
while it was being jettisoned overboard. The North Koreans cap-

138

tured the *Pueblo's* crew of eighty-two men after they surrendered their ELINT (electronic intelligence) vessel.

During the first half of that same year, the Israeli submarine *Dakar* sank in the Mediterranean, with a loss of sixty-nine men. The French submarine *Minerve* also sank in the Mediterranean, and another fifty-two men died. On 22 May, the USS *Scorpion* (SSN 589), while four hundred miles southwest of the Azores, suffered a "hot torpedo" disaster resulting from an explosion of the MK-37 device that became inadvertently "enabled" in her torpedo tube. The naval court of inquiry determined that, after the torpedo was ejected from the *Scorpion*, the fully armed weapon almost immediately struck the submarine at roughly amidships. The *Scorpion* dropped below her crush depth and sank in ten thousand feet of water. Ninety-nine American sailors died.

Within three days of the loss of the *Scorpion*, the Soviet experimental nuclear submarine K-27 experienced a major accident, the details of which have never been fully revealed. Five servicemen on board the submarine were killed immediately, and the remaining crew members were hospitalized with serious injuries. Attempts were made to repair the submarine, but the damage was extensive and the vessel was finally scuttled, with its nuclear fuel still on board, near the island of Novaya Zemlya, east of the Barents Sea.

▼

CAPTAIN HARRIS WAS CALLED to Washington, D.C., at about the time that the Hawaiian police pulled me over for having a cracked front windshield. It was just a tiny crack, I told the burly officers as they filled out the citation. It was minute, almost impossible to see. Besides, I added, there are so many people in Hawaii who drive cars with *no* front window.

"You have a cracked window, sailor. You have to fix it," the larger policeman said, handing me the ticket.

"But, officer," I pleaded, "I'm going to sea shortly, and we may be gone for a long time. Can I fix it when I get back?"

"Ain't no big thing," the man said with classic Hawaiian non-chalance, "just stop by the local precinct and they'll clear you for your voyage." He smiled and added, "No problem, bruddah."

As I drove around Honolulu and looked for the local precinct, Captain Harris was being interrogated by Admiral Rickover about the *Viperfish*'s mission. Rickover had recently emerged victorious in his battle with Secretary of Defense Robert McNamara on the matter of developing a new class of submarine that later became known as the *Los Angeles* class. Now, however, Rickover was focusing his attention on the *Viperfish*.

His questions to Captain Harris were specific and intense:

What is the mission of the *Viperfish*?
What is the submarine looking for?
Who is in charge of the mission?
Who allocated the money for the mission?

As instructed by the directors of the Deep Submergence Office of the Pentagon, Harris deferred the first barrage of questions. Rickover asked more questions, and Harris deferred those. It was a "damned if you do/damned if you don't" situation for the captain; he could not disobey direct orders from the Pentagon, and he could not follow direct orders from the admiral. By the time Rickover finished his blasting and dismissed Harris from his office, the captain was on the long list of unfortunate individuals who had incurred the wrath of a man famous for a remarkably long memory, combined with a vindictive pattern of retribution.

In the engine room of the *Viperfish*, a new chief petty officer, Gary Linaweaver, reported on board to take over Rossi's job as leader of the Reactor Control Division, a change all of us welcomed. Linaweaver was bright and savvy, a veteran of the *Nautilus* and *Scamp*, as well as the Polaris submarine *Vallejo*. He brought us a wide range of knowledge about nuclear reactor control systems and operations. Best of all, his jaw muscles didn't pulsate in a distracting manner when he talked to us, his biceps didn't throw the fear of God into anybody standing nearby, and he didn't look like he was ready to kill someone.

The day before we were scheduled to leave Pearl Harbor, I discovered that somebody had painted over the large white "E" and "655" that had been prominent on the side of the *Viperfish*'s sail.

"Where's our 655?" I asked Kanen, as I walked across the brow and fired off the traditional two salutes to the colors and the topside watch.

"Painted over, gone," he said, simply.

I studied the sail and discovered that a random pattern of dark gray camouflage paint also had been added to the black color over the sail and to the remainder of the superstructure.

"We are becoming invisible," I commented as I climbed through the hatch leading to the control center.

The stage was set for our departure. After nearly two years of preparation, we were ready to take the *Viperfish* to sea on a mission that still remained a complete mystery to almost the entire crew. There were no speeches by the captain or other officers about the days ahead—no rallying about a goal that must be reached or an objective that must be accomplished. The nukes were expected to keep the reactor systems on line for propulsion power and electricity. The men of the forward crew were expected to navigate and perform the standard submarine operations necessary for getting us safely there and back. The civilians in the hangar...well, nobody knew what the civilians in the hangar were going to do other than lower the Fish, look around the bottom of the ocean, and bring up the Fish when they were finished. At the time of departure, for all I knew, we were heading for the coast of Australia to study underwater reefs.

Although I did not know it at the time, the mission of the *Viperfish* finally had become defined by a mysterious and unexpected disaster in waters far from the Hawaiian Islands. For the first time since I had reported on board the submarine, we were now on our way to search the bottom of the ocean for a specific top secret target that appeared to be extremely important to the

United States. Our mission changed from one of establishing our
capability of finding, undetected, any deep-sea target of choice to
a defined and urgent mission of locating a specific target created
by events and chosen by men far beyond the knowledge of the
crew. This single fateful event in a distant ocean had transformed
us from a vessel with remarkable capabilities to a submarine and
a crew with a mission that would now take us into the deepest
waters of the Pacific.

We had prepared to leave Pearl Harbor, however, with spirits
battered by the Vietnam War demonstrations and the turbulence
across the country. As my parents had warned me, anybody
wearing a uniform was viewed as a part of the Vietnam War. I had
felt the resentments in the Berkeley bookstore, I had seen the
obscene signs directed at me while I was in uniform, and I had
watched young protesters throw garbage toward my car when
they spotted my uniform.

We strongly resented these demonstrations. An attack against
our uniforms was viewed by us as an attack against our country,
and the protesters, therefore, were a kind of enemy. Also, it
seemed that the protesters were attempting to destroy the values
that most of us felt were important and to move us toward eradi-
cation of our society's structure. The defense of that society was
the very reason why most of us wore the uniform.

The antimilitary sentiment created a mood of frustration that
further shortened everybody's temper in the tight submarine
quarters. We all had a sense of irritation and professional dissatis-
faction because of society's widespread absence of approval. We
knew little and could say nothing about our Special Project operation that might clarify the value of our work on the *Viperfish*, so
nobody in the civilian world could understand why we would
endanger our lives with a mission that couldn't possibly be more
important than the war in Vietnam.

We cast off our lines and pushed away from Pearl Harbor with
the dejected feeling that we were serving an uncaring society. We
also left with great caution, reinforced by the recent deaths of more

than two hundred submariners around the world. Although we had received no official naval announcements about the multiple disasters, we knew that machinery had failed, submarine crews had possibly erred, and capable men had died. Even our involvement with a project that presumably had minimal potential for military conflict (although none of us was sure that this was the case) seemed to place us at considerable peril. We knew we were at risk just by the very nature of our work. The little wooden sign hanging in Captain Harris's stateroom–"O God, thy sea is so great and my boat is so small"–took on new and poignant meaning as we approached the great expanse of the Pacific Ocean.

During the departure, I perched in front of the reactor control panel to scrutinize the various meters and watch for anything that could shut down the plant and stop our submarine dead in the water. I adjusted the reactor's control systems as we cleared Hammer Point, passed the Papa Hotel demarcation line, and powered across the surface of the ocean.

In the cockpit of the sail, high above the *Viperfish*, Lieutenant Pintard was waiting for word from the captain. The large and jovial officer of the deck, studying the calm ocean in front of our bow, was on the lookout for any debris that could strike the tops of our periscopes during the submerging operation ahead. Captain Harris stood at his side and scanned the myriad of ships off the west coast of Oahu, while the two lookouts announced the various bearings and distances of the ships passing by. Behind the four men, the American flag flapped vigorously in the wind, the sound blending with the noises of churning ocean water and the distant rumbling sound of our propulsion system.

"All ahead standard," Pintard ordered into the microphone under the rim of the cockpit. His voice carried down to the men at the diving station below and into the engine room's maneuvering area where we monitored the reactor and propulsion system. At the sound of the order, Marc Birken and Jim McGinn immediately began cranking their wheels toward the left to open the throttles.

The whine of the turbines increased in intensity, and we all duti-fully placed the black plastic sound guards over our ears to protect our hearing. From that moment on, if anybody in the engine room wanted to talk, he had to shout. For the most part, however, there was no conversation; we just sat in front of our panels and watched the maze of meters displaying the various conditions of the reactor and electrical systems throughout the boat.

At the top of the sail, Captain Harris leaned over the side of the cockpit and studied the white wake that began to boil around and behind us as we answered the bell and increased our speed.

"Ten seconds from the order and look at that!" he said, obvi-ously impressed.

"Nuclear power," Pintard said, reflecting on the obvious.

"No clouds of black smoke, no delay."

"Rickover would love it."

"Let's take her down," the captain said. He stepped through the hatch and began the long climb down to the control center.

"Aye, aye, sir," Pintard said as he and the two lookouts made a final scan of the horizon and the world around them.

"Strike the colors and clear the bridge!" Pintard ordered.

The two lookouts immediately lowered their binoculars, removed the American flag, and scrambled down the ladder. Following behind them, Pintard moved his large frame down the sixty-foot ladder with the knowledge that he would not see the sunlight again for at least two months.

Inside the submarine, the captain watched the ocean ahead of us through the starboard periscope as the three men jumped off the ladder into the control room. One of the lookouts reached up to the lanyard attached to the hatch and vigorously pulled on it. With the resounding noise of steel against steel, the hatch slammed tightly against the pressure hull and closed off our last remaining opening to the outside world.

"Control room hatch shut and dogged, sir!" the lookout hol-lered as he spun the wheel on the underside of the hatch.

The chief of the boat, a short, sandy-haired man named Philip O'Dell, grabbed the microphone hanging near the diving station and announced, "Now, dive! Dive!"

As the chief's voice echoed throughout the submarine, the lookouts eased into their cushioned seats and pushed forward on their airplane-like control wheels. The ballast control panel operator flipped switches across his panel to open valves and flood our external ballast tanks, thereby increasing the weight of the boat and sinking us down into the water. The *Viperfish's* bow dipped, and we assumed a 20-degree down-angle. The gentle rolling movement of the surface waves changed to the motionless sensation of losing contact with the rest of the world.

"Like hanging in outer space," Svedlow commented from his seat next to me.

"Inner space," Lieutenant Katz corrected him from his engineer's seat behind us. "At least we ain't going to be rolling any more, and nobody's going to get sick down here."

We moved several hundred feet below the surface, not deep enough to worry about excessively increased ocean pressure but sufficiently deep to keep us below any surface ships. If we suddenly had to surface, collision with a moving ship was not likely. We would hear their engines and screws from several miles away and adjust our course accordingly.

It was vastly more difficult to identify stationary objects on the surface, however, because we couldn't see them and we couldn't use our active sonar, which would give away our position to anybody listening. Our sonarmen, sitting in their "sonar shack" room near the control center, monitored the noises of various cruise liners passing above us. Undoubtedly, the ships were filled with vacationing tourists, admiring the approaching island of Oahu, who did not have a clue that a submarine holding 120 men was tracking them from below.

Once we leveled out at running depth, Richard Daniels relieved me from the reactor control panel watch, and I was free to roam about the boat for the next eight hours. Because three qualified reactor operators were now on board, my life for the next two months would be composed of a seemingly endless number of twelve–hour segments, each consisting of four hours of watching the reactor control panel and eight hours of sleeping or wandering around the boat and wondering what to do next. During this entire time, we would remain submerged, as we waited for the Special Project team to gather whatever information the Fish could find and hoped that something good came of it all.

We had come to accept that the captain and other officers would not tell us in what direction we were heading, where we were going, and what we were going to do when we got there. All of us knew we were going to be searching for something that was extremely secret. Surprisingly, nobody was much bothered by the fact that we were provided with no information. The crew, especially those in the engine room, were to remain almost entirely out of any tiny information loop that might exist. We did not need to know anything about the Special Project in order to do our jobs.

Each man had his own regimen to counteract the boredom during his hours off watch. I had packed stacks of novels and correspondence courses in French and chemistry from the University of California into my bunk locker, and I planned to spend much of my free time reading or preparing lessons. The *Viperfish* also had about seventy–five full–length motion pictures stored in the dining area; after the evening meal, each movie was shown twice for the men off watch. Many of the movies were first–run features and were thoroughly entertaining, but many others had never reached the ticket–buying public and had subtitles accompanying strange stories that made little sense. Whether the movie was good or bad, we generated the usual continuous observations about everything, from the way an actress walked to the lines her lover whispered in tender moments of love. Nothing occurred in any movie that was too small or too trivial to deserve at least one comment from a member of the crew.

On the second day out, one of the cooks discovered an old, dusty two-hour film reel showing landings of Regulus missiles. The *Viperfish* had previously fired Regulus missiles as her main purpose in life, and there was considerable interest in seeing the results of our boat's old missile days. Prior to the discovery of the movie, nobody on the boat was aware that the Navy ever landed missiles. We logically assumed that once the missile had been fired, it was simply destroyed on impact, along with the target. We all pulled up seats at the dining room "theater," turned out the lights, and hollered for the ancient film to roll.

The entire movie was a repetition—the same thing, over and over. First, we saw the blue sky and an occasional palm tree or two waving in the breeze. Suddenly, two tiny specks appeared in the distance and approached the island at high speed. After a few seconds, we recognized a winged Regulus missile, with lowered wheels, closely followed by a Navy jet with a pilot struggling to control the Regulus with radio signals. The missile's engine was off as it maintained a high-speed glide in the direction of the runway.

It was a silent movie, and there was no hint as to the source of either the missile or the jet. They both just came out of the sky, from specks to full size in about thirty seconds. No landmarks identified the island, which appeared to be a remote uninhabited coral reef. Throughout each sequence, the pilot of the jet endeavored to keep his slow-flying airplane from stalling, while he worked to bring the Regulus safely to the runway. We guessed it was a reclamation process of sorts, to salvage the Regulus missiles and perhaps to lower the cost of each test firing.

As we silently watched, the first effort failed miserably. The missile, too far to the left of the runway, was aimed almost at the cameraman before it frantically moved to the other side in a manner that landed it straight into the trees. The next missile, controlled by another pilot, had a better chance. It appeared to be lined up correctly; however, just before its tiny wheels touched down, it began to waver and finally nosed into the asphalt in a spectacular crash that disassembled the thing all the way down the runway. The third missile touched down nicely, its wheels spinning furiously, and we all cheered just before it lifted back into the air and began bouncing wildly down to the end of the runway, where it crashed into the lava rocks. The fourth missile appeared briefly and then suddenly disappeared out of sight, presumably crashing into the ocean.

By the time the fifth pair of specks appeared, we were all taking bets on the chances of chaos versus a successful landing.

"He's looking good! He's looking good!" Doc Baldridge hollered.

"He's going to take out the cameraman!" Chief Mathews yelled.

"Five bucks says it'll crash!" the cook called out.

"Five to one!" somebody else said.

"You're on!"

"Oh my God, look at that!"

"Bring it back to the left! It's off course!"

"It's too high!"

"Now, it's too low!"

"Dumb goddamn pilot!"

Another Regulus missile bounced and spun its way down the runway and finally disassembled into a heap of smoldering metal.

"Skimmer non–qual puke pilot!" was the usual final observation as money changed hands.

Finally, about five landings later, one missile actually came safely to an upright halt and the ocean around the *Viperfish* reverberated from our cheers. An hour and a half later, five or six more missiles landed safely, and we were left speculating about the award that the photographer must have received for filming so many missiles coming right at him.

The cook finally turned off the projector. Some of the crew drifted off toward their racks for a few hours' sleep, while others wandered off to the far corners of the boat to assume their watches. A half hour later, the next group of men coming off watch assembled in the crew's dining area for snacks and the watching of a special movie, starring the United States Navy, titled *Attempted Landings of Regulus Missiles, Using Jets.*

We continued to move through the ocean toward our mysterious destination, the engine room pulsating with the power of a reactor running at nearly 100 percent to drive the propulsion turbines at top speed. From the plummeting temperature of the ocean water, it was apparent that we were moving in a northerly direction, but none of us knew whether we were heading west toward the Soviet Union or east in the direction of the United States. On the fifth day, that issue was settled as we entered the Domain of the Golden Dragon.

I had not heard of the beast. At the time of the first announcement, I was lying in my rack and studying a lesson related to the conjugation of a long list of French verbs. If I completed ten lessons before our return to Pearl Harbor, there was a good chance that I could soon finish the course and be one step farther along the tortuous pathway to a college degree. It would not be difficult, I reasoned—just conjugate the verbs, memorize the vocabulary, pull out my portable typewriter, and assemble the lesson for the professor in his office at Berkeley. Immediately after I memorized the fourth verb on the list, Chief Mathews made the announcement over the ship's 1MC loudspeaker.

"Now, attention all hands! We have a sonar contact, bearing 275 degrees, one mile off the port bow, closing on the *Viperfish* at twelve knots!"

I slammed the book shut and yanked back the curtain covering the opening to my rack.

A sonar contact closing on the *Viperfish*? A torpedo?

I stuck my head out into the passageway and looked around, half expecting to see men running to battle stations. Nobody was running anywhere, and the only sign that anyone else had heard the announcement was the presence of several other heads looking out from their racks. I reasoned that it must be some kind of torpedo fire–control drill.

Mathew's voice came out over the loudspeaker system again. "Now, sonar reports the contact has attached to the boat! The contact has attached to the boat!"

This was getting weird very fast. It had to be a strange homing torpedo, I thought, or maybe a type of mine that was somehow attached to the *Viperfish.* I jumped out of my rack in a rush and began to dress quickly, as I listened for a call for surfacing, for battle stations, or for somebody to do something.

"Now, we have entry!" the chief's voice carried the urgency of the situation. "We have confirmed entry of an unauthorized biological form into the wet bilge of the boat."

The opening to the wet bilge, on the decking immediately next to my rack, was covered by a steel grating that spanned the hole. Unfortunately, at that moment, I was standing on top of the steel grating. I froze and slowly looked straight down into the bilge, my mind struggling with the concept of an unauthorized form somewhere below me. Standing at the bottom of the wet bilge was one of our enlisted men, Willie Washington, looking straight up at me, his eyes wide open and filled with fear.

Immediately, he began climbing up the ladder as fast as his arms and legs could move. He was shrieking, "There's a biological something coming in! Lemme outa here!"

I held the grate open for him as he flew out of the wet bilge and disappeared down the passageway without looking back to see what kind of biological form might be chasing him. I lowered the grating and stood directly on top of it. Looking down into the hole, I wondered how anything attaching from outside our boat could migrate through the maze of pipes into the bilge.

And that was when Chief Mathews made his final loudspeaker announcement.

"Now, all skalliwags and non-quals, all pukes and others who have not crossed the 180th meridian, I am authorized to announce that the Golden Dragon has gained entry into the *Viperfish!* The Dragon will be immediately convening a golden tribunal in the crew's dining area. All non-quals and other pukes without a certified document granting entry to the Domain lay to the crew's dining area for determination of guilt and justice, according to the Honorable Code of the Golden Dragon!"

The line was long, the trial was short, and the justice was swift. We entered the darkened dining area, one at a time, to find ourselves staring at the face of a huge Golden Dragon with fiery illuminated eyes and a belly that looked remarkably like that of the nuke machinist mate, Joaquin Santos. Paul Mathews had been assigned as the Golden Assistant for the Dragon; there was no defense except useless whimpering pleas for leniency. The creature itself served as the honorable judge, the prosecuting attorney, and the jury; the Dragon's word was absolute and would yield to no appeal.

I was found guilty of all charges. General malfeasance, corruption, multiple gestures of disrespect to the Golden Dragon, and other compelling but undefined improprieties were included, and the sentencing occurred immediately. A quick swig of the Golden Brew was the punishment, a matter ably attended to by the Golden Assistant, Chief Mathews, who provided me with a ladle filled with the foulest, greasiest, oiliest soup I had ever tasted. As I gulped the solution, large quantities spilled onto my dungaree shirt, leaving me with a musty rotting odor unknown to the civilized world. My stomach immediately rejected the entire mess. With cheers from the crew and an identification card certifying me to be now worthy of the Golden Dragon's domain, I was ordered to leave the court before the tribunal reversed its honored and lenient decision. I returned to my rack, where French books took second place to a quick but thorough shower and a change into clean dungarees.

After moving through the Golden Dragon's 180th meridian, Chief Mathews expanded my education in naval lore with his story about the Golden Dragon. Since the time that Greek and Roman sailors guided their fragile vessels on the high seas, the benevolence of mythical gods was believed to be essential for survival and success. As the centuries passed and science advanced, the improved understanding of the challenging forces at sea–weather, waves, and unsettled shiftings within the human mind–diminished the importance of the gods. Only two remain in

control of these elements today. Although King Neptune continues to dominate sailors crossing the equator, the more fearful
Golden Dragon of the international date line, the supreme serpent
controlling the 180th meridian in the mid–Pacific Ocean, generates
greater respect from sailors entering its waters. Stretching thousands of miles east of the Kamchatka Peninsula and north to the
Aleutian Islands, the violent and turbulent seas within the control
of this mythical creature are known by all men of ships and submarines as the Domain of the Golden Dragon.

Continuing our presumably westward journey to enter the icy
waters of the Soviet sector, we pushed through the ocean with
wide–open throttles for several more days. We finally approached
a destination of sorts, somewhere, I guessed, near the Kamchatka
Peninsula. The announcement came with an abrupt change in our
bell, the first new propulsion order in more than a week, that
bolted Marc Birken to attention with the order, "Slow to one-third!
Do not cavitate! Do not cavitate!"

Marc rapidly cranked his throttle wheels nearly shut as everybody sitting in the maneuvering area of the engine room looked
up at the cavitation indicator lights. The noise from the tiny bubbles spinning off the screw made a cracking noise that could be
heard for miles. It was essential, if we were to avoid detection by
others, for us to slow the screws and rig the ship for silence.

Since "do not cavitate" was now a standing order for the engine
room, it was apparent to me that the captain suspected that
somebody, out there in the ocean, might be listening for us.

The captain and executive officer also spread the word for us to
do everything possible to maintain silence. Although we could
talk, watch movies, and move around the *Viperfish* in a relatively
normal manner, we were careful to avoid slamming the steel
hatches separating the compartments and to avoid dropping anything on the decking.

Of greatest importance was the garbage. Any light bulbs in the
debris ejected from the *Viperfish* would implode with a bomb–like
detonation that could be heard for hundreds of miles. Silence was

imperative. Garbage bags were checked and double-checked. It was almost as if we had started tiptoeing through the dark spaces of a stranger's house because somebody, probably armed with an arsenal of lethal weapons, could be nearby—awake and listening for the sounds of an intruder.

We shifted in the chairs of our watch stations as these thoughts penetrated our consciousness. The unknown nature of the listening force added to its ominous nature and made it seem more powerful and frightening. Moving slowly and silently through waters that were likely within the Soviet sector, we could almost feel the presence of something or someone above us or around us—listening, waiting, ready to take action against us if we were detected. The crew's morale, already burdened by the problems of the society we had left behind, was further weighted by this new threat. Nobody speculated about what would happen if we were detected, but the subject persistently haunted us while we concentrated on the cavitation monitor and silence.

Chief Morris obviously felt it as much as the rest of us. That evening, he snapped at one of the crewmen, "There's a flashlight in the engine room with dead batteries. Didn't you guys run the PM [preventive maintenance] last week?"

"I'm sure we did, Chief," the electrician answered, calmly. "Which flashlight is it?"

Glaring at the man, the chief stuck out his jaw and said, "I'm not going to tell you. You're going to have to find it yourself."

The man looked at the chief but restrained himself from making any comment. He roamed throughout the engine room as he tested each flashlight one at a time. It took him a half hour, but he finally found the bad light and replaced the batteries.

The rest of us jumped on the chief from that point on. In the subtle manner of submarine crews everywhere, we delivered our message without running afoul of the military chain-of-command structure. When anyone asked where something might be located, the answer, almost always within earshot of Chief Morris, was always an impudent, "I'm not going to tell you. You're going to have to find it yourself."

At that point, we still had almost two more months on patrol. There would be no escape for the chief. He would receive the same message, over and over, wherever he might wander throughout the *Viperfish*. He learned fast, however, and never pulled a "you gotta find it yourself" trick again.

More than a week after leaving Pearl, and nearly two years since the *Viperfish* had started her long journey as a spy submarine, we reached a destination that was unknown to most of us. The SOBs in the hangar compartment prepared for the search. They checked and double-checked our coordinates from the ship's navigation system and compared the data with the information they had been given in Hawaii. Working diligently, they began to prepare the Fish for the complex process required to lower it into the high-pressure ocean.

Finally, they started lowering the Fish down the hole and out through the belly of the *Viperfish*. It was a cooperative effort by Lieutenant Dobkin, Robbie Teague, Captain Harris, and the cluster of civilians. They all tossed out ideas and orders as they eased the Fish, one foot of cable at a time, into the ocean on the start of its journey that would take it miles away from our submarine.

We did not linger around the hangar during this time, so that the SOBs could do their work without our intrusion. Hoping that something worthwhile would come of it, we managed the rest of the boat. It was apparent that our ability to function as a seagoing submarine in matters of military defense was highly limited with the expensive Fish trailing several miles below us. We could not quickly change course, we could not speed up or slow down, and we were unable to change our depth abruptly without destroying the search pattern or damaging the Fish. We were like a military aircraft, flying through the middle of a battle zone at dangerously slow speeds with flaps extended, landing gear down, and controls frozen.

The *Viperfish* was vulnerable, and everybody knew it. Even though the Fish was nearly twenty thousand feet below us, it had to be carefully pulled by its cable so that it would remain only a few feet off the ocean floor. The entire operation was extremely delicate, and its success depended on our moving slowly, systematically, and deliberately at all times.

During the first few days of the search, my biggest worry was the consequences of any flooding. The Fish and its cable likely would be destroyed during any emergency surfacing action or by a sudden loss of propulsion power resulting from any problem in the engine room. I found myself forcing these thoughts from my mind during the long hours of sitting in front of the reactor panel and wondering who was out there listening for us. All of us worked hard to concentrate on the meters spread across our panels.

After two weeks of quietly moving back and forth across our search pattern, the noise from the first explosion hit our submarine. It was clearly audible to all of us, a distant "whomp!" followed by a long period of stunned silence from our crew.

"What the hell was that?" I asked Brian Lane. Brian and I had been sitting side by side in front of our control panels for the past three hours, as we watched our meters, puffed on cigars, and tried to stay alert despite the monotony and boredom of our tasks.

Lane turned in his chair and looked at me. For a moment, I thought he hadn't heard the noise–his eyes didn't seem to register the enormity of an explosion in the ocean thousands of miles from land. He looked inappropriately relaxed as he spoke the hang–loose Hawaiian vernacular of the day, "Ain't no big thing, bruddah."

I stared at him. "No big thing? Jesus Christ! We're in the middle of the ocean, Brian," I said. "There's not supposed to be anybody else out here."

"It could be from a thousand things," he said, dismissing the more ominous implications.

"Or it could be somebody has found us."

"Survey ships, war games by our guys, fishing fleets detonating fish to the surface, it could be anything."

Glancing back at the reactor control panel, I scanned the meters and looked for anything even slightly abnormal as more explosions went off. I adjusted the reactor control system and shifted around in my chair.

The man of the house is looking for the intruder, I thought.

Behind us, Lieutenant Katz called the control center, asked a couple of questions, and listened carefully. "The captain doesn't know what the sound is," he said, hanging up the telephone. "The sonarmen think the noise is probably coming from a sonobuoy dropped by something–an aircraft, a ship, or maybe even another submarine."

Another explosion went off, and all of us waited for the next one.

"Goddamn!" I said as I put my clipboard down and waited.

"Somebody out there is exploring the thermoclines," Katz said, referring to the layers of water created by virtue of their different temperatures. A layer of cool water next to warmer water causes the deflection of sonar waves; objects, such as submarines hiding on the other side of the thermocline, are concealed from detection by ships on the surface. To improve the chances of finding deeply submerged vessels, floating sonobuoys eject explosive charges that drop deep below the surface. When the charge sinks to a predetermined level, it detonates and the sonobuoy broadcasts any reflected echoes to a receiving ship or aircraft.

It is a tricky business because of the "tunnel effect" that echoes the explosive sound back and forth down the tunnel for many miles and confuses everybody about distances. If we were sitting at the end of a long thermocline tunnel, an explosion from five or ten miles away could sound like it was right outside our hull. Unfortunately, there is no easy way to determine whether or not a tunnel is present. We had no way of knowing if the explosions were from a distant source or right outside our boat.

10

MAN OVERBOARD!

IN EARLY 1968, a Soviet Echo II submarine designated PL–751 ("PL" for *podvodnaya lodka*, or submersible boat), with ninety men on board, returned to her home port of Vladivostok on the eastern coast of the Soviet Union. For a prolonged duration, she had been on station within range of U.S. targets, and her captain and crew were looking forward to several weeks of well–earned time ashore. According to the timetable of Soviet submarine deployment, she was to be relieved by her sister ship, currently undergoing preparation and scheduled for departure at the Vladivostok submarine base.

To the distress of the men on board PL–751, they were informed on arrival that their relief ship had developed mechanical problems and would not be able to deploy. PL–751 was forced to stock up on food and supplies, cast off her lines, and immediately return to sea for another prolonged period on station in the Pacific Ocean.

As she cleared the Sea of Japan, her cavitating screws broadcast their characteristic signature to the listening SOSUS array below. The sounds, as well as her northeast direction of movement, were duly noted by the U.S. Defense Intelligence Agency (DIA) monitoring specialists who were thousands of miles away. Cruising north of the Japanese island of Hokkaidō, PL–751 passed over the deep Kuril Basin at the edge of the Sea of Okhotsk, navigated between the Kuril Islands, and finally powered into the open waters of the Pacific. She maintained full 30,000 SHP (shaft horsepower) from her twin shafts and dual reactors. Crossing the undersea Shatskiy Rise and approaching the Emperor Seamount, she moved in the direction of her patrol sector within missile range of Midway and the Hawaiian Islands.

When PL–751 reached an area in the northern mid–Pacific Ocean, a region pinpointed at exactly 35° N, 172° E, a violent event destroyed the submarine's watertight integrity. The precise nature of this event is unknown, but it was possibly the result of an explosion from hydrogen gas during battery charging operations, an explosion during the handling of missile fuel, or human error as the fatigued crew pushed themselves and their submarine beyond the limit.

The captain and crew immediately struggled to save their ship as she took on increasingly high–pressure water and slid deeper into the ocean toward her test depth. Within several seconds of the time when she roared past her maximum designed safe depth, the waters of the northwestern Pacific Ocean were filled with the popcorn noises of rupturing pipes and bulkheads as the PL–751 accelerated through her crush depth and delivered her entire crew to the bottom of the ocean, 19,200 feet beneath the surface.

The Soviet Union made no announcement to the world about the sinking of the PL–751, and the United States released no information about the sounds that had found their way into the SOSUS microphones at the bottom of the Pacific. During the next several days, American intelligence forces monitoring Soviet ship and aircraft movements recorded an unprecedented number of radio message intercepts originating from Petropavlovsk-Kamchatskiy on the Kamchatka Peninsula and Vladivostok. Also,

during this time, satellite and other highly classified sensing systems recorded a dramatically increased number of Soviet naval
and air search operations traversing the routes of U.S. task forces
patrolling in the North Pacific.

▼

The explosions, carrying up and down the thermoclines, continued to vibrate the hull of the *Viperfish*, but we tried to ignore the
noises and the implications of their presence. Occurring at irreg-
ular intervals for several weeks, they disrupted our sleep, frazzled
our nerves, and made everybody feel miserable. During this time,
we relentlessly pursued our search of the ocean bottom. As the
weeks stretched into a full month with no sign of success, morale
plummeted even more. The most ominous sign of widespread
discontent was the oppressive silence that began to emerge
throughout the *Viperfish* as the Fish found nothing, the explosions
continued, and our hope for success waned. When the crew was
happy, everybody groused about everything; when the crew was
depressed, silence prevailed. The *Viperfish*'s crew was becoming
silent.

As we roamed our search area, the civilians and Special Project
crewmen debated the best way to scan the bottom of the ocean
for our target without missing any areas. Some previous experience with towed devices, similar to the Fish, had been docu-
mented in the archives of U.S. search projects, such as that by the
USS *Mizar*, the oceanographic research ship that had found a
nuclear bomb off Spain, but there was almost no experience with
a submarine towing miles of cable.

Is it best to move in a straight line back and forth across the
search area, they wondered, with the potential of losing the
"lineup" during each complicated turnaround procedure? Should
the submarine encircle a central point by starting with a huge
circle that gradually becomes smaller and smaller? Maybe the
circles should start at a central point and expand by ever-
increasing diameters. Or would it be better to make equal-sized

circles overlapping in a single direction that would result in a wide swath of searched ocean bottom, hopefully performed in such a manner as to rule out any missed areas.

There were no books on the subject and little information beyond the *Mizar* data. Most of us were vaguely aware of the *Mizar*'s successful operations, which included finding the USS *Thresher* in 1964, but the *Mizar* was fundamentally different from the *Viperfish*: she was a surface craft. Searching the bottom of the ocean in a vessel heaving around on the surface is, in some ways, more of a challenge than it is in a submarine that remains at a fixed depth below the surface.

At least, in a submarine, depth control is usually possible to predict and maintain. Because it was essential for the Fish to remain a specific distance above the bottom of the ocean, in order to prevent its destruction by contact with terrain irregularities, precise submarine depth control was mandatory. Alternatively, if the *Viperfish* pulled the Fish too high above the bottom, its ability to "see" anything below it would be compromised. As long as no emergencies developed that would require sudden changes in depth, a silent submarine was clearly the vessel best suited for a secret search of the ocean's bottom.

The speed of the vessel also dramatically affected the altitude of the Fish above the ocean floor; if the *Viperfish* inadvertently slowed for a few seconds, the Fish could easily sink and be destroyed against rocks or ridges. Cable length had a nearly immediate effect on the Fish's altitude, and careful control of the spool rotation was of top priority. Reactor power and turbogenerator power were essential to operation of the Special Project's computer system that analyzed information from the Fish. Finally, the *Viperfish*'s buoyancy, depth, and direction, which were controlled by the ballast control operator, the planesmen, and the helmsmen, required close communication and teamwork.

Success, however, continued to be elusive. As time passed, we all became increasingly frustrated. We experimented with different methods of moving the boat, and we varied circular patterns and Fish elevations. Each new trial consumed days at a time and resulted in nothing.

After all of these failures, Robbie Teague brought a stack of stunningly clear 8 × 10 black–and–white photographs to the crew's dining area to show us life at twenty thousand feet below the surface, complements of the Fish. Bizarre bat–like structures stuck out from the bodies of some fish, and others had ornaments clinging to their faces. Other structures resembling slugs lay on the bottom; Robbie called them sea cucumbers. As we passed around the pictures, we expressed appropriate interest in the fauna, complimented Robbie's photography and the clarity of the images, and asked if the civilians had found the object of our search.

Robbie's smile faded. "Not yet, but we're still looking."

"Are we still circling, or have we started a new pattern? If we can't find it here, why can't we look somewhere else?" Richard Daniels asked, his voice sounding tense.

"Because this is where it's supposed to be," Robbie said, almost inaudibly.

"Tell us what it is, and we'll become more enthusiastic. Is it a UFO?" Daniels asked.

"They don't have me in the loop. Can you understand that?"

"A nuclear warhead?"

"It's secret, guys, secret."

"Nobody on the *Viperfish* knows what we're looking for?"

"Nope, nobody I know around here. I just develop the pictures, and—"

"Why is this thing so important?"

"It's classified, it—"

"Right, right, but if we can't find it, then where it's supposed to be doesn't mean much."

"Okay," Robbie said softly, "you're right. However, if we keep looking, we do have a chance. And they tell me it's important."

Robbie gathered his pictures in the silence that followed and, without another word, returned to the hangar compartment–his diplomatic mission of fostering Special Project enthusiasm a notable failure.

As we cruised around and around and back and forth and as morale continued to slide, a shocking event occurred one morning in the crew's dining area. We were all eating freshly cooked oatmeal, when one of the forward crew machinists violently spit the cereal all over the dining area table and jolted the men around him.

"Goddamn it all, where's the cook?" the man hollered as everybody began to examine their own cereal.

"Right here," Marty Belmont said, looking concerned as he walked up to the table. "What's the problem?"

Marty was a chubby, pleasant little fellow who worked as hard as anybody on the boat and did a good job. His work was especially important because the meals were almost the only variability in our day–to–day lives, and good food meant a happy, or at least a happier, crew. The budget for food on submarines exceeds that of any other branch of the Navy. Regularly taking advantage of that fact, Marty tried to make the food as tasty as possible.

"Marty, there's goddamn worms in the goddamn cereal!" the machinist hollered, spitting out more food. Immediately, everybody in the dining room, including myself, simultaneously blasted food from our mouths. The tables were covered with a layer of partially chewed cereal.

"Jesus Christ, Marty, don't you check for bugs in the food?" another man yelled.

"Did Robbie give you these animals from the bottom of the ocean?"

I spit out some more food and carefully examined the bowl of cereal in front of me. Thousands of tiny white worms, crawling among the grains of warm cereal, exactly matched the color of oatmeal–a perfect camouflage, unnoticed by the rest of us. It occurred to several of us, as we groused and grumbled and generally felt miserable, that the cereal had actually tasted pretty good, a little meatier than usual perhaps, but the flavor was definitely unique.

Marty gathered up the bowls, his face distressed, as he reflected on the ruins of the morning meal. "I'm sorry, fellas. They must have broken into the grain. I cooked the cereal but I guess I didn't get it hot enough. Damn little buggers shoulda died."

We all stared at the man, speechless.

Finally, one of the men stood up and handed Marty his bowl. "Even *dead* worms don't belong in the cereal."

"I'm doing the best I can," Marty said, wiping down the tables, as a couple of the other galley crewmen joined him to clean up the mess covering most of the tables.

From that day on, the phrase, "I'm doing the best I can," became synonymous with the ever-increasing numbers of important things going wrong in spite of the best intentions.

The search continued for another two weeks, until even the normally enthusiastic civilians in the hangar became discouraged. Robbie didn't bring any more pictures to us, and the men throughout the *Viperfish* stopped speculating about the object of our search. A feeling of profound frustration and gloom descended on everybody. The explosions outside our hull were similar to Chinese water-drop torture; each one wasn't that loud but added together, day after day, the noise created a mental state of continuous uneasiness.

As our second month under water began, I found myself slowly feeling more and more claustrophobic. None of us had seen any sunlight or sky since the day we left Pearl Harbor. After each four-hour watch, the dilemma of nowhere to go and nothing to do became a problem. I had passed the time by completing French lessons and reading a couple of books during the first month at sea, but now I found myself becoming restless after reading just one or two pages–it was getting increasingly difficult to concentrate. My French lessons were becoming much more of a challenge, and it took all the effort I had just to sit down and concentrate on trying to understand bits and parts of the language.

The final blow came shortly after I started working on the last paragraph of a full page of carefully typed French. The typing of my correspondence course work had taken most of my free time during the preceding several days. Moving from one word to the next, I struggled to avoid mistakes, looked up each incomprehensible French idiom, penned in the proper accent marks, and corrected the inevitable errors that slipped through in spite of it all. As I endeavored to clarify the spelling of a particularly strange French word in the last part of the final paragraph, a large hydraulic valve above me abruptly cycled with a loud whoosh. A thick glob of grease dropped from the valve directly onto the part of my typewritten page sticking out of the typewriter.

I stared at the oil as it slithered down the single-spaced sentences. Watching the typewriter ink smear as the oil diluted the letters, I felt my head begin to pound. I ripped the page from the typewriter, shredded the paper into the tiniest pieces I could manage, and cursed France and everybody in Europe. Then, I steamed down to the crew's dining area to watch another half hour of Regulus missiles crashing down runways on a deserted atoll in the middle of nowhere.

After almost seven weeks of fruitless searching with the background noises of sonobuoy explosions echoing up and down Soviet thermocline tunnels, Captain Harris finally decided to bring in the Fish and head back to Hawaii. We began the prolonged process of reeling several miles of cable into the *Viperfish*. Cruising back and forth with our Fish out–a mother ship with her very long and delicate umbilical cord–was not an exercise that made us feel particularly useful, especially so because we had failed to find anything worthwhile. Most of us looked forward to stowing the miserable device and reconverting the boat into a more maneuverable non-Fish towing vessel. We hoped that we could now at least try to function like the military ship we were supposed to be.

During the hours of reeling in the Fish, a powerful storm began to build in the waters stretching across the North Pacific. We were at a depth of three hundred feet, where surface wave activity should not affect us more than 90 percent of the time; on that day, we entered the 10 percent portion where rules didn't apply. It was a slow-roll type of movement, nothing that would make us think about hunting for Ralph O'Roark but enough to let us know that nature was stirring up the surface. The noises of sonobuoys stopped at the beginning of the storm, and everybody began to feel better as the huge spool outside our pressure hull continued to reel in the Fish. Finally, to our great relief, the civilians stowed the Fish in a corner of the hangar and the captain ordered the *Viperfish* to pick up speed and begin clearing out of the Soviet sector.

I relieved Richard Daniels from his reactor watch shortly after we began to accelerate in the direction of Pearl. We had to shout to be heard above the whining of the propulsion turbines and reduction gears, which were thirty feet away from the maneuvering area. I gathered the information from Richard about the reactor, now running at full capacity, and pulled up a seat in front of the control panel. Brian Lane sat next to me, manning his complex electrical control panel. To my surprise and in contrast to his silence of the past several weeks, he now became more talkative.

"We're running low on fuel," I said, as I gathered data from the meters filling the panel in front of me. There is no fuel gauge, per se, to pinpoint when the nuclear reactor requires a new uranium core, but data from multiple operational sources leave no doubt about the remaining fuel.

Brian turned and smiled at me. "Enough to get back?" His smile faded. "Right?"

"Enough to get back," I reassured him. "If my calculations are correct."

"No gas stations out here—"

"No uranium stations," I corrected.

"No shore-power cables to hook up to the battery."

"Nope, gotta rely on the reactor. Lucky for the forward pukes that they have the nukes to get them back."

"Thank God."

Lane then turned in his chair and looked at me. His eyes seemed to stare through me, but he smiled in a way that was strangely out of sync with the general mood throughout the submarine.

"You can't get to me," he said in a matter–of–fact tone. I watched him as he turned back to his panel and began scanning his meters.

The phrase was a familiar submariner idiom. "You can't get to me" speaks the essence of being a submariner. It is a statement that says, even in the cramped quarters and continuous press of close human contact, even when there are worms in the cereal and detonations in the ocean, nothing is allowed to get under the skin. "You can't get to me" said it all: nothing bothers me, I am a professional, and there is no way anything that is said or done will be a problem for me.

Lane said it at the wrong time, however. He watched his panel while I looked at mine, our ears enclosed by the plastic sound guards that shut out the screaming machinery around us. After noting more data on my log sheet, I glanced sideways at the man and wondered why my friend and shipmate had said something so far out of proper context. I finally dismissed the matter with the speculation that he must have misunderstood–the shrill noise of turbines drowning out what I had said.

About that time, when I was feeling about as grouchy as almost everybody else, the EOOW decided to quiz me. A tall man, Lt. George Sanders was moving up through the ranks of nuclear-trained officers, but he had an officer–elitist attitude. His trace of an "I am better than you" approach contrasted sharply with the leadership capabilities and personalities of the other submarine officers who fostered our respect by earning, rather than demand-ing, it. He got on my nerves as he paced back and forth behind Lane and me when we were on watch, and I was never quite sure what he was going to say next.

On this watch, he was irritating me more than usual. So, when the quiz began, I clenched my teeth, crossed my arms across my chest, and stared at the reactor panel.

"Okay, Dunham," he said from behind me, "you're cruising along at four hundred feet."

Consistent with the range of appropriate responses of an enlisted man to an officer, I respectfully answered, "Yes, sir."

"Okay. Now, the ship begins to sink."

"Yes, sir, the ship sinks." This would not be difficult, I thought, just a matter of the ship sinking.

"*Begins* to sink!" he shrieked. "You now have two choices. You can save the reactor or you can save the ship."

"Yes, sir." I was sure I would have more choices than two.

His voice became icy. "Well, Dunham, what are you going to do?"

"I'll save the ship, sir," I said, not having a clue as to where his line of speculation was leading.

"Right, that is correct. Very good." I adjusted my ear protectors in the hope that his voice would blend in with the turbogenerators.

"However, Dunham," he continued, "you will save the reactor if I tell you to save the reactor."

With that, Lieutenant Sanders had reached his goal. Even though I might want to save the ship, he, as an officer, would force me to do something contrary to training and common sense. It was a power thing. What I should have said at that point was something like, "The choice is yours, sir, because you are the EOOW."

I felt a flash of irritation at the whole line of questioning, so I blurted out, "No, sir, I would not save the reactor."

He stopped pacing the deck and stood directly behind my chair. "You would save the reactor if I told you to," he said forcefully.

My irritation rose. I jotted a couple of numbers from the reactor panel onto my clipboard. "No, sir. I would save the ship, but I would not save the reactor."

His voice climbed an octave. "You would save the reactor if I told you to!"

"No, sir."

I noticed Brian sinking down into his chair. He was trying to be as inconspicuous as possible.

The lieutenant became livid. "You would if I told you to!" he yelled, bits of sputum flying in all directions.

"No, sir," I answered politely. "I would not be inclined to save the reactor, sir."

He began to hyperventilate. A couple of enlisted men standing near the maneuvering area quickly walked away, probably searching for a place to hide. I gnashed my teeth, grabbed the reactor clipboard, and noted some additional information in my logbook as Sanders finally sat down, his face red with anger. I put the clipboard down and wondered if I was going to be court-martialed for refusing a hypothetical order. From my perspective, the entire issue was the result of everybody being annoyed about everything, the failure of our search mission, and the effects of nearly two months of submerged duty. But, for Sanders, it was personal, an enlisted man's insolence, and something, by God, that was going to be taken to Lieutenant Pintard immediately after the watch.

Ten minutes after I finished the watch, Pintard took me to the hangar compartment, now quiet, and spoke like a father to an errant son, "Dunham, Dunham, Dunham…"

"Well, he was a bit out of line, sir," I said.

Pintard smiled. "Lieutenant Sanders is an excellent officer, and next time just tell him what he wants to hear."

"Hypothetical orders–"

He raised his hands to stop me. "If Mr. Sanders wants you to save a mermaid swimming to the moon, just tell him you will do everything possible to save the bitch, okay? This is a submarine, but there is a military structure that needs to be followed."

I agreed, and that was the end of the issue; however, a new phrase, "You will if I tell you to!" entered the lexicon of the *Viperfish*'s crew. It was repeated a hundred times during the days ahead, usually within earshot of Lieutenant Sanders and always in the tone of an authoritarian out of control. If somebody said, "I'm really not sure I'd want to swim in the Ala Moana harbor," the immediate, reflexive response would be a hollered, "You would if I told you to!"

Because there is no way that any man on a submarine can escape the "pinging" (verbal barbed wire) of the crew, an early lesson of submarine life, for an officer and enlisted man alike, is that there is a price to pay for being obnoxious. The barrage of pinging from the entire crew can become incessant; when somebody with an inappropriate attitude is trapped with the crew, this can eat him alive. Wherever he walks, from bow to stern, other crewmen (officer and enlisted) are everywhere. They sleep above and below him; they sit at his table; they eat meals and watch movies with him; they use the head and take showers next to him.

If the word is out that he has brought any form of grief to one of the crew, retribution follows—a dig here or there, a phrase, anything that conveys displeasure—and it will not let up.

Two months is a long time, and there is nowhere to hide. Officers are as much at risk as enlisted men. From the cook serving protein–enriched cereal—"doing the best I can"—to the chief ordering his man to "find it for yourself," to the officer who orders "you'll do it if I tell you to," they will find no mercy from the crew. The pinging continues without pause until enough time goes by that everybody finally forgets the issue or until some redeeming act from the accused brings forgiveness and peace.

Two days later, when I passed by the radio shack, one of the crew angrily handed me an official Navy bulletin recently transmitted to the *Viperfish*. The bulletins were passed around the boat on rare occasions and served as a kind of Navy-oriented newspaper. After climbing into my rack and pulling the curtain, I turned on the light and scanned the front page. Anything would be more interesting than French lessons.

The first story reported the tale of an enlisted Navy man who was found guilty of using LSD. The LSD had caused him no problems except for prolonged staring sessions, and he seemed to do fine except for repeated, unpredictable flashbacks. On one such flashback, the man apparently thought he was an orange; the accompanying editorial warned of the dangers to nuclear reactor operators who think they are becoming fruit.

Because I never used drugs and didn't know of anybody on the *Viperfish* with any kind of a drug habit, I moved to the second article. This one was written by the captain of a nuclear submarine somewhere in the world who had purged most of the nukes on his ship for various reasons that seemed to have little merit. The article pointed out, however, that Adm. Hyman G. Rickover was quite satisfied with the action, was *happy* with the action, and the editorial warned us to stay on our toes, or we too might be at risk for a purge. As I remembered the NR Board debacle and began to feel gloomy at the thought of a Mao Tse-tung purification on board our submarine, I became aware of the *Viperfish* sliding into a steep and sustained down-angle.

I have never liked the feeling of our boat pointing her bow toward the bottom of the ocean. In most cases, a down-angle is a transient process carrying little risk. The helmsmen push forward on their Republic Aviation control wheels, and the entire vessel rotates forward into a downward slide. The duration of the down-angle affects the psyche of the entire crew. The steeper the down-angle, the greater the anxiety, until it becomes a waiting game—waiting for the down-angle to stop and for the submarine to level out. Depending on speed and buoyancy factors, a submarine can point down for only so long before something dramatic happens.

Outside the control station, the men had no information about the depth of the submarine during down-angle maneuvers, and no announcement indicated how much deeper the *Viperfish* was going. It was like being a passenger in a diving airliner that had no windows, with predictable results on the enclosed humans: a fine sweat covering the skin, a hand tightening its grip on the side of the chair, and irritation demonstrated by spontaneous small movements of annoyance.

When is the dive going to stop? How far down are we going to go?

Other thoughts, private thoughts, moved through the minds of the men riding the submarine down, thoughts about test depth and crush depth, thoughts about pressures at the bottom of the ocean, and sobering thoughts about survival. It was essential, we all knew, that the destination depth not fall below the ship's maximum test depth. In a steep dive, the time it takes to pass through the test depth and reach the crush depth is a matter of only a few seconds.

In submarine school, we had been told that submarines in the American fleet will often take steep down–angles under many operational scenarios. It happens all the time, it is normal. "The conning station knows what it is doing, it will not overstress the ship," we had been told. There is no need for panic, everything is under control.

Fine, but how long does the dive continue, and at what point would it be appropriate to start wondering about our depth?

I ripped aside the curtain of my rack. Looking up and down the passageway, I checked for anything that seemed unusual. The boat was definitely pointed in a steeply downward direction, and there was no indication that we were going to level out or move into an up–angle at any time in the near future. The off–watch crew was scattered throughout the berthing area, arms and legs protruding into the dark passageways, mouths rumbling out a symphony of snores. Several of the men began stirring restlessly as the down–angle increased a couple of degrees and the submarine seemed to accelerate her dive.

I swung out of my rack, pulled on my dungarees, and hiked up to the *Viperfish's* diving station to investigate.

At 0300 the control center was only dimly lit by glowing red pinpoints of light on the electronic panels–the compartment was fully "rigged for red." The room was unusually silent, and everybody looked grim. Captain Harris paced back and forth next to the lowered periscopes, Commander Ryack leaned across the railing and scrutinized the gauges over the shoulders of the two helmsmen. Chief Mathews and Petty Officer Michael Davidson, wearing life jackets, stood next to the ladder leading up to the sealed overhead hatch. With thick belts encircling their waists and steel chains, ready to be latched to railings on the outside deck, hanging at their sides, they were preparing to climb the ladder. I stared at them as I tried to understand what they were going to do.

I turned to Sandy Gallivan, standing at my side, and asked him what was going on. He looked at me, his face tense, his words strained.

"Problem with the Fish winch mechanism," he said quickly. "Gotta hold the boat in a down-angle or our Special Project operation is shot. Bates is keeping us steady at this depth with positive buoyancy, and we're moving real slow." He pointed in the direction of Joel Bates, the lanky ballast control panel operator, who was hunched over his chair, his eyes glaring at his depth gauges.

"Aren't we moving pretty deep right now, with the down-angle and all?" I asked.

"Even though we're about four hundred feet," he said patiently, "we're not changing depth because of the positive buoyancy. As we move forward, we float up by an equal amount, holding our depth steady. It is a delicate balance, and Bates is going crazy trying to keep us at four hundred. Mathews and Davidson are going topside to free the hydraulic lock on the Fish's cable reel. In about thirty seconds, we are going to surface."

"We're going to surface with a down-angle?" I asked.

"With a down-angle," Sandy confirmed, looking unhappy. "At least we're not dangling a Fish below us."

Mathews and Davidson rechecked the thick belts holding their rail chains and looked up the ladder at the control room hatch as Philip O'Dell grabbed the microphone to the loudspeaker system.

"Now, surface, surface, surface!" Chief O'Dell's voice bellowed from speakers throughout the submarine.

With the rapid movements of practiced experience, the men in the control center flipped the switches controlling the high-pressure ballast air system. As the roaring compressed air blew water out of our ballast tanks, we rapidly ascended–the bow of the *Viperfish* still strangely pointing down by about 20 degrees. We broke through the surface of the early-morning ocean, and the helmsmen immediately opened the control-room hatch connecting to the sail. The thin form of Gerry Young raced up the ladder in front of Captain Harris. Both men scrambled to the top of the sail, and two lookouts followed closely behind. Mathews and Davidson remained next to the ladder in the control center, as they waited for orders to move out of the *Viperfish*.

From sixty-five feet above the deck, Young's voice crackled over the loudspeakers in the control center.

"Con, Bridge, how do you read me?"

"I read you loud and clear, how me?" Chief O'Dell called into his microphone.

"I hear you same," the speakers replied.

For about ten minutes, the captain and the OOD studied the waves around the *Viperfish* in the early morning dark as she plowed through the heaving waters. The freezing rain and wind, occasionally carrying blasts of salt-laden sea spray, whipped around the cockpit and blew into their faces.

The boat rolled vigorously from the cross-wave activity. The lookouts watched for lights of any approaching ships. The dark shape of the *Viperfish* would not be visible to the crew of another ship because we were running without lights, and there was always a small chance of collision with some random freighter straying out of the shipping lanes.

Commander Young's major responsibility as the officer of the deck was to establish the best possible course for the *Viperfish* and head her directly into the driving seas. Swells hitting the bow of the boat were easily traversed, but those striking the superstructure from abeam could cause severe rolling. He ordered several course changes during the first few minutes to move the *Viperfish* into the best direction through the waves. As each wave rolled out of the dark with an almost predictable regularity and approached the bow, we lifted up smoothly to ride over the top.

The captain had a bigger problem. Chief Mathews and Petty Officer Davidson were about to leave the security of the boat to walk on a slippery submarine deck. Everybody was aware that we were more than a thousand miles from the nearest land, and there was nobody nearby to help if we had a problem.

Inside the control room, Mathews and Davidson climbed to the top of the ladder. Dragging their rail chains behind them, they stopped just below the open hatch to the sail. Again, they paused and awaited orders.

"Mathews, Davidson, lay topside, into the sail!" the captain's order finally crackled down from the control room loudspeakers.

The two men quickly disappeared through the hatch into the dark interior of the sail, their chains clattering behind them. Within the sail, they turned on their flashlights to light up the door leading to the outside of the sail structure. The chief yanked up on the handle and swung the door wide. As it slammed against the outside steel, torrents of rain and roars from the black ocean stunned the men.

"Jesus" was all Davidson said, softly under his breath. As the junior enlisted man, he would faithfully follow his chief into the hostile night. He would say nothing more but, rather, concentrate on the job awaiting them and ignore the energy hammering the world around them.

Waiting for their final orders from the captain, Mathews and Davidson clutched the bar inside the open door and tried to see out into the night. High above their heads, the captain, the OOD, and the lookouts continued to scowl at the powerful forces surrounding the boat.

The captain's deep voice finally rumbled down to the sail from the cockpit: "You're clear for the topside deck!"

The two men immediately stepped out through the sail door and clamped their short chains to the railing carved into the steel deck. Beginning to inch forward slowly and clutching the handrail on the starboard side of the sail, they dragged their chains behind them as they progressed toward the hydraulic pipes ahead.

"I can't see a goddamn thing!" Mathews growled to Davidson as he brushed the rain from his eyes and shined his flashlight into the night.

"Nothing to see but the goddamn freezing rain!" Davidson hollered back over the roar of the ocean. They rounded the front of the sail and prepared to move across the deck, Mathews leading the way in the direction of the hydraulic system's valves.

Without warning, a rogue wave loomed like a huge black mountain two hundred yards in front of the *Viperfish* and began rolling directly at the submarine's heaving deck.

The four men in the cockpit simultaneously saw the massive shape that dwarfed the boat and seemed to become increasingly larger. Driven by the winds and tortured by the forces of the sea pulling up into its face, the black wall of water roared in thunderous slow motion, the crest topped by foaming whitewater higher than the top of the sail. The lookouts hollered their warning. The OOD and the captain immediately tried to save the men on the deck below.

"Get back inside!" Young's voice blasted urgently from the top of the sail.

"Get into the sail!" the captain hollered. "Get inside, now!"

Young grabbed the microphone communicating into the control center and hollered, "Come right 20 degrees!"

The helmsman in the control center instantly turned the *Viperfish* farther to the right. The bow, moving slightly to the new course, pointed directly into the wave that seemed to grow like a powerful creature, a living thing preparing to devour the vessel and the men who challenged its waters.

"Come right another 10 degrees!" Young screamed into the microphone, as he tried to point the *Viperfish* directly into the powerful wave so that she could bisect and ride over it.

"Right, 10 degrees, aye, aye, sir!" the chief of the boat called back, and the helmsman responded with the rudder change.

The men on the deck turned and raced for the safety of the sail. Davidson reached it first, his chain now ahead of the chief. He frantically unlatched his clamp and leaped through the door, while Mathews hollered, "Go! Go! Go! Go!"

The wave hit the *Viperfish* head–on and consumed her bow. Crashing high over the outstretched bow planes, it foamed across the top of the bat–cave hump and finally roared across the deck toward the sail. Just as Davidson turned to reach for his shipmate, the decking around him shuddered from the wave's impact. Water flooded over the top of the sail and into the cock–pit sixty–five feet above the ocean, drenched the four men, and then roared down the long ladder. It almost washed Davidson back out the door.

A solid column of seawater crashed through the open hatch of the control room, flooded the decking, and soaked everybody in the area of the diving station. On the deck outside the sail, Mathews held his breath as the wall of water crashed into him. Burying him beneath its violence, the wave forced him away from the door and broke his grip on the sail's handrail. It slammed him against the deck and finally accelerated him toward the stern. Frantically, he reached toward his belt to grasp the chain that strained with the weight of his body dragging the clamp along the steel rail.

The clamp suddenly broke free from the rail. As the rush of water carried Mathews into the ocean, he struck the deck with a final glancing blow and disappeared toward the churning screws of the *Viperfish*.

Davidson, scrambling around inside the sail, tried to stand up again. He grabbed the hinges of the door and looked out into the night for Mathews. His broken flashlight washed out the door with the water clearing from the sail. His fingers clutched the inside railing as he leaned outside the door to search behind the *Viperfish* for any signs of a light.

"Paul!" he hollered at the top of his lungs, his eyes moving to the foaming sea that roared past the sides of the boat. He called the chief's name again, but he knew there would be no answer. He took one last desperate look before finally backing into the sail, his mind numb with the shock of losing his shipmate.

"Man overboard, starboard side!" he screamed up to the four men at the top of the sail. "The chief is gone!"

"Man overboard! Man overboard!" Young's urgent voice bellowed down into the control room loudspeakers as the captain and the lookouts shined their lights toward the foaming white water beyond the stern of the boat.

Inside the control room, Young's voice immediately hollered over the loudspeaker, "All back emergency!" to the helmsmen. "Right full rudder!"

We had performed drills like this a hundred times. Remembering the routine, I raced to the starboard corner of the control room to grab the man–overboard bag, a large white duffel bag filled with life vests and other floatation equipment. I dragged it across the deck to the base of the ladder and dropped it into the water pooling in front of the periscope station. It was obvious that the bag would be of no help to anybody.

In the engine room, Billy Elstner spun the ahead throttles shut and rapidly opened the reverse throttles that rotated the screws in the opposite direction.

"Who went over?" a voice called from the other side of the control room.

"Jesus Christ!" Commander Ryack exploded furiously, his voice filled with rage. "It doesn't matter who went overboard, goddamn it! It is one of our shipmates and that's all that counts!"

"Are we answering the back emergency bell?" Young's voice from the cockpit filled the control room.

"Yes, sir!" O'Dell hollered into the microphone, "Answering back emergency."

The lights throughout the boat briefly dimmed as the men in the engine room drained steam energy from the nuclear reactor in their effort to halt the *Viperfish*. Sloshing in the water I moved away from the ladder in the control center and felt useless. The life vests inside the bag couldn't even be delivered to the ocean, much less to the man in the water, and he was already wearing a life vest. Further, the flashlights in the bag would be immediately lost in the thrashing sea even if we could toss them out.

While Commander Ryack spun the starboard periscope around to search into the night, the four men at the top of the sail, two on each side, leaned over the edge of the cockpit as they scrutinized the waters behind the boat. There was no sign of Mathews or his light in the surrounding darkness.

"I can't see anything out there," the OOD said with frustration.

"He's out there," the captain said. "We'll go ahead with the 'Y' and we'll find him."

"Control, bridge!" Young hollered into his microphone under the steel lip of the sail. "Chief Mathews is in the water behind us! Can you see him through the 'scopes?"

"Negative!" Ryack shot back. "Nothing!"

The rudder orders came, and we started to make a "Y" turn, a procedure well known to the men at the top of the sail. The object was to back the boat in a tight, rotating movement while keeping the man overboard in full view. Our biggest problem was that nobody had seen the chief since the wave had washed him away. Also, now that we were turning in the sea, the waves began hammering at us from directly abeam, steeply rolling the boat from the lateral forces.

A larger wave, fifteen to twenty feet high, slammed into us and and hit directly broadside. Roaring through the open sail door, it drenched Davidson with more freezing water. He considered closing the hatch but then decided to leave it open in the hope that he would see the chief as the boat continued to rotate. About that time, however, he realized that Chief Mathews might not be conscious.

"We're tracking the area," Young called down to the control room as the rolls became more prominent. Both lookouts cursed as they scanned the ocean behind the *Viperfish* for any sign of a light in the sea.

"Answering full back emergency!" from the engine room, as we felt the pulsating power of the screws stopping our forward motion.

"Turn on the running lights and set the fire–control watch!" the captain hollered, ordering the men in the control center to man the dead reckoning tracer (DRT).

Another wave slammed broadside against us and rushed through the open door of the sail. Again, a column of seawater roared down the control room hatch and flooded the control center.

"Close the fucking hatch!" the executive officer hollered from the periscope station. One of the enlisted men pulled down on the halyard and slammed the hatch shut. He then activated his microphone to tell the men in the sail that they were sealed outside the *Viperfish*.

"Bridge, control!" he called out. "We've taken water in control! The control room hatch is closed!"

The loudspeakers responded a quick acknowledgment.

At that moment, I was sure that Chief Mathews was lost forever. There was no way we could recover anybody we couldn't see or reach, a man under the pounding waves, probably a mile or more away from us, a man now freezing in the waters of the Soviet sector. Sloshing through the ankle-deep water, I dragged the man-overboard bag away from the base of the ladder. Small waves moved across the flooded decking of the control room with the movements of the boat, and I looked for a bucket to help clear the water.

"Grab some sponges and move the water out!" Chief O'Dell hollered, as we rolled another 30 degrees and salt water splashed onto the fire-control panels. The technicians responsible for the electronics systems raced up and down the passageway to turn off everything in danger of salt water contamination.

I grabbed a fistful of sponges and tried to soak up the water. The boat continued rolling, now more violently as we moved across the "Y" and lateral to the seas. More waves of water splashed against the electronic systems. O'Dell and Ryack, each manning a periscope, rotated them back and forth as they scanned the ocean behind the *Viperfish* for any signs of Mathew's light. Staring through the lenses into darkness, they saw nothing but the black of a violent, empty night.

Outside the boat, the metal door on the side of the sail repeatedly crashed against the frame of the superstructure. It sounded hauntingly as if Paul Mathews was out there pounding the *Viperfish* with a hammer and trying to get back inside.

"Do you see anything through the 'scopes?" the captain's voice called down to the control center.

"Nothing!" Ryack answered. "Goddamn it, nothing" His thumb remained poised on the TBT (target bearing transmitter) button at the base of the periscope handle, his eyes scanning back and forth.

"Bridge, this is the engine room!" Pintard called over the loud-speaker. "We are approaching the maximum bearing temperature limits for our backing turbines!"

"Keep your bell on!" Commander Young's sharp voice yelled down to the engine room.

"Where the hell is he?" Ryack said, moving the handles of his 'scope. "It's a goddamn hurricane out there—"

"I don't see anything, either," O'Dell said from behind his 'scope. "He's out there somewhere."

The speakers filled with another call from the engine room, Pintard's voice now more persistent. "We have exceeded our bearing and oil temperature limits for the backing turbines!"

"Keep your bell on!" Young's voice roared through our loud-speakers.

"Gotta get him on the leeward side," Ryack said.

O'Dell rotated his periscope again.

"Gotta see him, first," he said.

"Problem is, we may run over him before we spot him."

"Goddamnit…"

"How long have we been backing down?"

"Probably four or five minutes. It took us two minutes just to stop."

The speaker came to life again, the EOOW's voice urgent. "Bridge, engine room, the bearing temperatures are now—"

"Keep your bell on!" Young hollered again from the top of the sail. Although Young was standing the OOD watch, as the boat's engineer, he probably knew the limitations of his turbines better than any other man on board.

I mashed sponges into the water and wrung them into the buckets as we struggled to clear more water from the control center. We are going to do everything we can to save him, I thought–we are even going to burn out our propulsion turbine bearings.

Dipping the sponges into the water again, I cursed the persistent slamming sound of the unlatched sail door. The noise struck blow after blow on the minds of the men in the control center. We heard it as a repetitive call from our man, lost in the howling forces of hell that raged around us, pleading for the crew of the *Viperfish* to bring him back.

"You Can't Get to Me"

WHILE PRESIDENT LYNDON B. JOHNSON was denying plans to use nuclear weapons in Vietnam, the death toll of American servicemen reached the highest level ever in a single week (ending 28 January 1968) when 416 men were killed and 2,757 wounded in the battles at Khesanh and Langvei. This brought the U.S. casualty total in Vietnam to 17,296 killed and 108,428 wounded. Senator Edward Kennedy of Massachusetts, after returning from a trip to Vietnam as chairman of the Senate Judiciary Subcommittee on Refugees, charged that the Saigon government was infested with corruption and inefficiency. His brother, Senator Robert F. Kennedy of New York announced his candidacy for the Democratic presidential nomination; his platform included de-escalation of the Vietnam War and reversal of the "perilous course" of American policies.

A jury in Boston, Massachusetts, convicted Dr. Benjamin Spock and others of conspiracy to violate the Selective Service law. Another jury in Baltimore, Maryland, found the Reverend Philip F. Berrigan guilty of burning and pouring blood on draft records.

Meanwhile, Selective Service Director Lewis B. Hershey suspended occupational and graduate student deferments and expanded the draft, as military spending on the war approached $100 billion.

Secretary of Defense Robert S. McNamara informed Congress that the Soviet Union had doubled its force of intercontinental ballistic missiles (ICBMs) during the previous year, but he added that the policy of mutually assured destruction (MAD) would allow for an effective and overwhelming retaliation after any initial Soviet nuclear strike. The Soviet Union news agency TASS reported eleven Cosmos satellite launchings in a time span of only eight weeks. The 65-degree inclination angle of these and other launches suggested the stationing of nuclear bombs in orbit as a part of a multiple orbital bombardment system (MOBS) that could destroy American targets at will.

A U.S. Navy court of inquiry into the explosion and loss of the USS *Scorpion* suggested that the vessel had been damaged by a Mk 37 torpedo accidentally set off by stray voltage in its tube. Analysis of SOSUS records, examination of photographs, and reconstruction analysis led to the conclusion that a single torpedo had exploded, probably after homing in on the *Scorpion* after her crew released the device. Sabotage and collision were considered but ruled out. The submarine had been in a tight turn at the time of the explosion, her sail had blown away, and the crew had tried to surface by blowing the ballast tanks and planing up. The compartments began to collapse, and flooding was widespread, except in the engine room, before the *Scorpion* reached her collapse depth. After careful consideration of all available evidence, the court of inquiry finally concluded that "the identifiable debris does not lead to a determination of the cause for the loss of the *Scorpion.*"

▼

THE MEDICAL CONSEQUENCES of being lost at sea mark a relentless path from initial shock and terror to a final paralysis that destroys the victim's mind and body. The first few seconds, a time when there still might be hope for a rescue, bring a harsh reality–the frantic search into the howling night for the departing ship, the stinging of eyes from the blasting of the water and wind, and the fighting for breath as the foaming ocean tries to invade the lungs.

During this time, the light attached to the life jacket shines a weak beam into the night with an energy that determines nothing less than the fact of survival itself. For when the battery's energy becomes exhausted, the light will fail as the victim himself will fail. And, as more time passes, the victim accelerates his downward slide that weakens the muscles and begins to spread a deadly paralysis throughout his body. He finally moves into a deep and frozen coma as his hypothermic mind is mercifully shielded from being a witness to his own death.

When Chief Mathew's chain had pulled away from the rail and he slammed off the *Viperfish's* hull into the freezing ocean, his shouts for help were immediately extinguished by the roaring of the ocean and the howling of the wind. He checked his light–his only lifeline in the night–and his fists formed a death grip on his life jacket. Struggling to hold his head above the pounding ocean, he knew, as a matter of cold and practical reality, that the shouting of his voice and the waving of his arms could be heard and seen by nobody. He knew from the beginning that his chance of survival was nearly zero.

He massaged the light attached to his life jacket and thought about pulling it free so that he could hold it high, but he quickly abandoned the idea. What would he do if he accidentally dropped it into the sea? He looked down at the light frequently, taking some assurance that its white glow could possibly mean survival. Without the light, he would be a dark shape in a dark ocean, a figure that could not be seen and would not be saved from the cold waters. For he knew that when hypothermia develops–the dropping of temperature as the body cannot produce adequate heat–the mind slows, body movements weaken, and survival is no longer possible.

At the periscopes in the control center of the *Viperfish*, Chief O'Dell and Commander Ryack continued their intense search of the waters behind us as the boat shuddered from the waves pounding the hull. Every roll of the submarine generated another wave of seawater rolling across the deck of the control center and crashing against the electronic control panels that lined our bulkheads. Another call from the engine room about bearing temperatures was followed by orders to maintain the bell, continue backing, proceed with the search for Chief Mathews, and the temperatures be damned.

Captain Harris saw the first flash of light. He and the other three men were searching from their vantage point high above the *Viperfish* as the submarine completed her backing bell. By its nature, the "Y" maneuver led to the vessel moving perpendicular to the wave motion, which resulted in the steep rolling that hampered our efforts to clear away the water from the control center.

It was just a flash, a spark and nothing more, from the center of blackness.

"Sixty degrees off the port bow!" the captain shouted and pointed into the night.

"All ahead two thirds!" Commander Young immediately ordered into the microphone connecting to the engine room.

"Left full rudder."

"The light's gone, sir!" one of the lookouts said, his binoculars aimed at the area several hundred yards away.

"He's probably under water again," the captain said as the *Viperfish* responded to the new bell. "We'll just close in on the area of the light. Bring her around, Gerry," he said to the OOD.

"If we don't see the light again, we're going to take a chance on going right over him," Young said.

"Just keep him downwind of the boat," the captain said patiently.

From the control room, there was almost no information about the events topside. We knew that the chief was gone; we knew that the backing bell had either destroyed, or come close to destroying, the turbine bearings; and we knew that the *Viperfish* was now starting to move forward. The two men on the periscopes continued their search, but they were greatly hampered by the steep rolls tilting the periscopes from one side to the other, which prevented them from getting a fix on anything around us. Everybody in the control room worked in a state of stunned silence. As we continued to clear water from the decking, we kept hoping that some progress was being made from the top of the sail, but we also knew that a recovery under these conditions was extremely unlikely. After hearing the ahead bell and the rudder changes and then the all-stop bell, we waited for ten minutes while absolutely nothing happened. The final story of Chief Mathews came to us only later, in bits and pieces.

From the top of the sail, the men in the cockpit saw the light again, and then again, as the *Viperfish* completed the "Y" maneuver and came to a halt, upwind of the chief.

"Hang on, Mathews!" the captain yelled as the final approach was made. "We're going to get you!"

There was no answer from the chief as the deck party of lookouts and a thoroughly soaked and freezing Michael Davidson ventured out on the deck for the recovery. They threw lines from the boat in his direction and then threw more lines. Mathews did not reach out for them or move closer to the boat, and he did not respond. In the end, a man went into the ocean to bring him back.

Suddenly, the hatch above our heads opened, and a splash of water dropped into the control center.

"Stand by to bring him down the ladder!" Davidson hollered from inside the sail, and we all gathered around the base of the ladder to help.

Mathews was nearly unconscious when the men carefully lowered him, head first, down the ladder into our waiting arms. He was sobbing, speaking incoherently, and mumbling over and over, "I never saw the boat."

"It's okay, Paul," we told him as Doc Baldridge checked his abrasions, several of which were still bleeding. He had slammed against the boat's superstructure a couple of times when his chain separated, but he had no broken bones or serious head injuries.

We wrapped him in several blankets and moved him down to his rack, where the Doc repeatedly checked on him for the next two days.

He had been in the water only twenty to thirty minutes, but, for Mathews, those minutes had been an eternity. While in the ocean, before his mind began to fade and before his muscles developed the malignant paralysis of hypothermia, he was certain that he was going to run out of time. He could not see the boat, he could not know we were closing in on him, and he could not know there was still hope.

"Let's take her down," the captain said softly to the OOD at the top of the sail.

"Clear the bridge! Clear the bridge!" Young called out, and the men scrambled down the long ladder into the safety of the *Viperfish.*

"Dive! Dive!" the chief's voice was broadcast throughout the boat as hatches were shut and we angled down again, away from the fury on the surface. Dropping hundreds of feet, we returned to our quiet existence beneath the sea.

For the next two days, we conducted a mini-celebration of Paul's return and toasted the safe conclusion to his experience. He wouldn't shed his blankets. Staying in his rack most of this time, he seemed to be always cold, always struggling to return his body temperature to normal. His response to our kidding–to such questions as, "How was liberty?"–was a silent gaze. We were aware of a fundamental change in him that had resulted from his experience. He told us no details about the event; he wouldn't talk with us, other than to tell us again that he had never been able to see the boat after his rail chain had broken away from the deck of the *Viperfish.*

We cruised slowly at about four hundred feet for the next three days, our bow again pointing steeply down and our speed slowed by the difficulty in maintaining a stable depth because of the problem with the hydraulic mechanism. We waited for the storm to pass, and we accepted the dangers of an unstable submarine. There was no consideration of any more trips to the surface until the waters returned to a relative calm. When the conditions were finally right, we surfaced again and the problem was readily resolved. Soon, we were back at four hundred feet, level and steady, en route to Pearl Harbor, still six days away.

Having a "doctor-patient" relationship with Paul Mathews, Doc Baldridge never did share much information with us about his treatment of the man. He gave his patient some bourbon from tiny medicinal flasks reserved for such times, and he kept the chief wrapped up. Doc never said much about his psychological state or the mental effects of a near-death experience. To me, Paul seemed depressed, but I also thought that Doc Baldridge was becoming depressed, as well as everybody else throughout the *Viperfish*.

Because we never saw much of Paul after his rescue, I asked Doc Baldridge what the problem was.

"Wouldn't you be a little shut down after something like that?" he asked me in return. His voice carried a little more anger than I think he intended.

"Of course," I said. "I was just wondering—"

"Paul's doing fine, but I don't have much time to spend with him since I have to work on the film badges, check the garbage gas measurements with our own oxygen levels, update everybody's records with—"

Holding up my hands, I tried to stop him. "It's okay," I said, "It's okay."

"There's not much more I can do here, on this boat out here," he said. "You know—"

"I understand, Doc," I said. "If you want to get off submarines, just put in a 'non-vol' chit and you're on your way. Just remember they're killing—"

"I know, I know," he said, exasperated. "They're killing four hundred men a week over there in the goddamn war, and a lot of them are corpsmen."

Eventually, we were all depressed. Paul lay in his rack, almost noncommunicative. The captain and the men working with the

Special Project were frustrated and feeling defeated. The nukes wondered why so much work was going into moving us back and forth, from one unknown place to the next, where we could fail and fail again. The entire morale of the *Viperfish* at this point consisted of gloom and doom, defeat and frustration. In that setting, Brian Lane started down his path of becoming internally lost at sea.

At the time, Lane and I had been standing our watches together in the engine room. Sitting side by side at our control panels, we controlled the machinery that provided propulsion power and electricity to the *Viperfish*. He was as depressed as the rest of us, but he started to develop a strangeness, beyond my experience or knowledge, that seemed to eclipse what the rest of us were feeling. We were all a little strange in many ways after being at sea, mostly submerged, for two months. I couldn't concentrate on French lessons or anything else; I was continually tense and irritable, neither of which was a part of my usual character; and I felt like I was just trudging along in doing my job–standing watch and sleeping, standing watch and sleeping some more. I didn't care much about the evening movie, and I was just working with the rest of the crew to get us back to Pearl Harbor. There, we would be able to blow off steam and forget about failed missions, the capture of intelligence vessels on the high seas, and the Vietnam–inspired disruptions of our society.

Starting the mid–watch that night, I took details from Richard Daniels about the condition of the nuclear reactor, logged the initial data on my reactor log sheet, and finally sat in the chair in front of the control panel. All routine, this watch was the same as all the others. Next to me, Lane took his watch from Svedlow, performed a similar function with the electrical equipment, logged his data, and watched his panel that controlled circuit breakers and other electrical systems. Behind me, Lieutenant Pintard and Chief Linaweaver paced back and forth as they watched over us and the engine room.

"Hey, bruddah, how's it going?" I hollered over the noise to Lane. I just wanted to open the door to any thoughts he might have about the nuclear system, our mission, or life in general. The four–hour watch ahead seemed like a very long time.

When he turned to me, he looked strange. I was about ready to tell him to knock it off, that he was giving me the creeps, when I noticed his hands were shaking. He said, "You can't get to me."

There it was again. Wrong comment, wrong context, simply the wrong thing to say.

"Nobody's trying to get to you, Brian," I said, watching the meters that monitored our nuclear reactor. "I just asked what's happening. Looking forward to seeing the wife and kids?"

He smiled and another strange look, an almost spacey look, came my way. I felt the hairs on the back of my neck beginning to rise.

"You guys can't get to me," Lane said.

I decided that the man was becoming too stressed out, so I turned my attention back to the reactor panel. Watching the meters and logging the data, I occasionally thought about how good it would be to see Keiko again.

Speaking to nobody in general, Lane began to babble in long sentences that didn't connect well. As he talked, I watched my panel, thought some more about Keiko, and wondered how soon channel fever would set in as we moved closer to the Islands.

Lane kept talking for another hour, until both Pintard and I implored him to be quiet. He was getting on our nerves, we said, and he wasn't saying anything all that profound anyway. Each time we said anything to him, he got that strange look in his eyes again and told us, "You can't get to me."

Finally, Chief Linaweaver had had enough.

"Lane, I'm ordering you to be quiet," he said tersely.

The strange look followed, the small smile of knowing a tiny secret appeared, and again he said, "You can't get to me."

At that moment, my friend, Sandy Gallivan, standing watch in the control center, squeaked a call through on the engine-room telephone to tell me about overhearing that there would be a flooding drill within the next five minutes. Of all the drills we hated the most, the flooding drill headed the list.

We were always aware that the *Viperfish* cruised above a defined crush depth, that our lives depended on preventing any inadvertent movement to that depth, and that flooding was the one event that could quickly take us to the crush depth. Because of that fear, we worked very hard not to think about it. Flooding drills, even on the rare occasions when we knew they were only drills, brought this awareness to the surface of our thinking and triggered the collection of fears that was part of the psychological territory of the Submarine Service.

Lane began to talk again, and the shaking of his hands became intense.

"Lane, for Christ's sake," I began with exasperation, "will you stop–"

At that instant, the roaring of incoming water drowned out all other noises.

Lieutenant Pintard jumped to his feet and grabbed his microphone as the loudspeaker above our head began blasting Billy Elstner's voice from the lower–level engine room into the maneuvering room.

"Flooding! Flooding! Lower–level engine room!"

Pintard hollered orders to isolate the leak. I stood up to concentrate on my reactor panel and watch for anything that could shut us down.

"Losing vacuum in the starboard condenser!" Elstner hollered, followed immediately by half the lights in the engine room shutting off and more alarms going off. The men in the control center instantly announced, "Surface, surface, surface!" and the *Viperfish* angled steeply upward. I glanced down the passageway and, with a shock that hit me like a physical blow, saw Lane running from the maneuvering area. His empty chair was swinging back and forth in front of the electrical control panel.

Immediately, without orders from Lieutenant Pintard and without comment from anyone in the area, one of our electricians, a big red–haired man named Tom Braniff, who was standing watch at the steam plant control panel, bolted from his watch station at the throttles and took over the electrical control panel.

As a couple of machinist mates chased Lane across the engine room, another jumped into the throttleman's position and answered the bell driving us up to the surface. Braniff began flipping switches across the complex panel, cross-connecting electrical circuits, and bringing life to our electrical system as the machinist mates shut down the leak. My reactor never twitched once throughout the entire process.

The machinist mates caught up with Lane near the watertight door at the forward section of the engine room just as Chief O'Dell announced on the loudspeakers, "Secure from flooding drill." Lane was shaking badly. He was trying to talk, telling them that nothing could get to him, nothing would be too much for him to tolerate. They took him to Captain Harris's stateroom and called for Doc Baldridge. Lane was relieved of his duties, and the corpsman started him on mild sedatives to calm him down for the remainder of the trip to Pearl Harbor.

The stress of our mission, compounded by the negative pressures from our fractured society, must have pushed Lane to the edge, I guessed. He must have known that he was becoming impaired long before the rest of his shipmates, who knew little about such things, could help him to seek treatment. Following a pattern that any of us might have pursued, he continued to try to perform his duties. He stood his watches even when the pressured speech pattern of the impending breakdown gave testimony to the problems lying below the surface. When the paranoia generated his wall of defense, preventing anything around him from "getting" to him, he was able to stretch himself to continue his work a little longer until he could return home to his wife and children and find comfort for his tortured soul. Brian Lane gave it his best shot. He tried with every coping mechanism that he had available not to allow his inner turmoil to stop him from fulfilling his assignment before the electrical control panel.

The final days of our run to Pearl Harbor pushed us further to the point of becoming intolerant of anything and everything. With Chief Mathews still recovering from his near tragedy and

Brian Lane walking back and forth with a half-smile and glassy eyes, we were all beginning to trudge to our watch stations. News bulletins told of more disciplinary actions against the men of the nuclear Navy by Admiral Rickover, more riots by students against our military, and expanding drug use throughout society. The world seemed to be falling apart.

The last news bulletin that I read before deciding to read them no more included an order "from the top" that no longer would qualified submariners be thrown overboard. This tradition had been determined to be too dangerous.

So, when Baby Bobbie's body odor finally "got" to everybody on the *Viperfish*, several men took corrective action by thoroughly saturating his sheets with talcum powder. The next time the man swung himself into his rack, a huge cloud of powder puffed into the air. This led to an instant fury that carried all the way to the chief petty officers' desks. Soon thereafter, we received a new directive–a direct order not to coat sheets with talcum powder, no matter how bad anyone might smell.

The attack of channel fever was especially intense. Most of us stayed awake for two days before arriving at Pearl. We finally surfaced several miles off Oahu and stationed the maneuvering watch. Leaving the nightmare of the Soviet sector behind us, we glided up the warm channel waters toward the submarine base. The traditional flowered lei was placed around our sail, and a boat delivered an admiral and a team of hospital corpsmen and doctors to our boat. As the admiral inspected the *Viperfish*, the medical personnel examined Mathews and Davidson. They took Lane into protective custody for ambulance transportation to Tripler Army Hospital, the first step in the process of ending his career in the Submarine Service. He would eventually receive a medical discharge from the Navy.

Our mission failure was symbolized by the absence of the broom tied to the top of our periscope. The broom represented a "clean sweep of the enemy to the bottom of the ocean"–a symbolic message of a successful mission, a declaration of victory that

had been used since the days of U-boats and conventional submarines. Without the broom, the approaching Navy brass would
know of the *Viperfish*'s failure before we even tied up to the pier.

Keiko was finishing her master's degree and preparing for our
wedding in Los Angeles, so Marc Birken and I again faced the row
of colorful and beautiful people with nobody waiting for us. I
walked toward the brow to leave the boat and was stopped by an
enlisted man in charge of distributing mail.

"You are Petty Officer Dunham, right?" the man, a pimply-faced,
short fellow with a whining voice, asked.

"That's right," I answered tersely.

"Good," the man said. "I'm supposed to hand deliver this to you
from the Honolulu Police Department, and I need you to sign
here." He handed me an envelope covered with official police
markings, and I signed the receipt for the delivery. "And, this brick
is for you, too," he said, tossing me a stack of sixty-two letters from
Keiko, one for every day I was gone.

I opened the Honolulu Police Department envelope and discovered a warrant for my arrest. I had failed to answer their directions to fix my defective front windshield, the warrant said, and if
I did not turn myself in they would come and get me.

Shortly after Chief O'Dell announced that Paul Mathews was
"non-volunteering" from submarine duty, I discovered that somebody had stolen the speed-shifting gearbox from my '55 Chevy
while we were at sea. Feeling a mind-numbing anger begin to
emerge, I wandered into the submarine barracks and tried to figure out how to get a couple of drinks in Waikiki without a car
and without the risk of being arrested.

Marc, sitting on his rack, was waiting for me. He looked serious.

"Hey, Rog, did you see the news?" he asked.

"No. And I'm not sure I want to see the news, Marc. Who's riot-
ing about what, now?"

"They just showed it on TV. Robert Kennedy was assassinated
last night by some slimy character known as Sirhan something-
or-other."

I looked at him in silence. Then, I turned and picked up my seabag. Slamming it against my rack, I started cursing the entire civilized world with genuine passion. I cursed the Honolulu Police Department, the thieves in the night, the banana-smoking druggies, the assassins, the student activists, and I cursed the nonexistent targets at the bottom of the ocean.

When I was finished, Marc congratulated me for my eloquence and mentioned that he wouldn't be around for the next *Viperfish* patrol. He was finishing his tour in the Navy, he said, and going back to Ohio, a place with fewer disruptions, to sail on Lake Erie where waves did not exceed six inches. Also, he planned to go back to school–to a peaceful institute of higher learning called Kent State University, whose students knew how to behave themselves. He was going to be a civilian, and he hoped that the *Viperfish* and her crew would have better luck on the next mission.

We both knew that the depleted uranium core of the *Viperfish* would allow for only one more mission to the distant waters of the Golden Dragon. Soon, she would be taken out of active service to undergo nuclear reactor refueling operations at Mare Island, California. I would have just enough time for my wedding in Los Angeles and a honeymoon in Canada before our final voyage to the North Pacific to continue our search for the mysterious target at twenty thousand feet below the surface of the sea.

12

THE FINAL SEARCH

No sunlight illuminates the impenetrable black water concealing the secrets at the bottom of the North Pacific Ocean. At a latitude of 35° N, light rarely penetrates the surface of the sea for more than a hundred feet on the clearest days, and it never reaches through the three miles of water separating surface craft from the mud below. At twenty thousand feet below the surface, there is only a somber dark peace far removed from the turmoil of the world above.

Entering the silence with the noise of her own destruction, the submarine PL–751 fell like a freight train to seventeen thousand feet below her crush depth. Breaking up from the forces of the high–pressure water, she spilled her lifeblood of men and equipment as she accelerated to the bottom of the ocean. The larger parts of the submarine crashed into the ocean floor with such force that their retrieval by any surface craft, struggling over the pieces in years to come, might be technically impossible. As the larger central section rolled on its side in a final agonal movement beyond the control of any human being, the sediment stirred by the impact slowly began to settle across the lifeless remnants. The once-powerful Soviet instrument of destruction had been trans-formed into a collection of broken and silent objects.

In the silence of the months that followed, nothing disturbed the remaining bodies of the Soviet sailors contained within the hull of the destroyed vessel. More than four tons of pressure com-pressed every square inch of skin on reaching the bodies through openings in ruptured pipes and destroyed bulkheads that had buckled and caved under such extremes of pressure.

Outside the broken ruins of the PL-751, the outstretched bones of a skeleton, lying on the mud, could not touch a large steel Fish that came from more distant waters and slowly glided past the area. As the Fish moved closer, controlled by men working in another world five miles from the scene of destruction, her bril-liant flashing strobe pierced the black shroud covering the ocean floor. With a subtle change in direction, the Fish turned and directly approached the remains of the disaster. Methodically, it searched for the evidence that had been awaiting its arrival with the infinite patience of the dead.

▼

AS I PREPARED TO LEAVE the *Viperfish* for Los Angeles, a new sense of urgency descended on the submarine. After Captain Harris returned from another trip to the Pentagon, activity increased, day and night, on the *Viperfish*. The captain provided no announce-ment on his return—no information to clarify the *Viperfish*'s pur-pose, nothing about the final search looming in her future. Yet, at this time, when we had been hammered by the events of the past two months, when two of our crew were gone from us forever, when antimilitary sentiment was rampant throughout our fami-lies and society, there was not a man on board who was not ready to go out and search again.

Stepping up preparations for another voyage gave further sup-port to these feelings and rallied us around the Special Project, with all its secret implications. One more search was all we asked for. Even though Harris divulged nothing about the Pentagon meetings, a whirlwind of activity stirred the air from the wardroom all the way down to the most junior enlisted man on board.

Lieutenant Pintard, in charge of the Reactor Control Division, cracked his whip on Chief Linaweaver–get the equipment ready to go, finish all the necessary preventive maintenance work, and ensure that nothing will shut us down on our next patrol. Linaweaver turned around and cracked the whip on the qualified reactor operators, and we, in turn, blasted the two new operator trainees, whom we called Dickie-Doo and Robbie Too, with stern admonishments to "get qualified, you non-qual pukes."

As the result of these actions, a new esprit de corps roared throughout the boat. We yanked open electronic panels, recalibrated gauges and meters, and poked hissing vacuum hoses into electrical drawers holding circuits exposed to microscopic amounts of dust. As the men in the wardroom planned the details of our next patrol, the rest of us worked day and night to make sure that the equipment would get us there and bring us back.

Another matter, thought about by all the nukes but discussed by none, was the matter of our diminishing fuel. No matter how much work we might do in preparation for our next effort to find the mystery target, the *Viperfish* was running out of "gas." The heat from nuclear fission could be produced only by a reactor with enough uranium to sustain the reaction, and Rickover's engineers were about to yank the *Viperfish* from the pool of operative U.S. nuclear submarines. I had done the calculations before shutting down the plant after our first run, and I knew the allowances necessary for starting up the reactor again. The news was okay but not great. We would have just enough power to get to our previous location in the Pacific and return, if we didn't spend too much time with any significant diversions or emergencies.

Not worrying about such mundane matters as nuclear fuel, the Special Project civilians and officers also worked around the clock to prepare the cable, load the stores, pack replacement parts for the Fish, and get ready for departure, now barely four weeks away. The entire crew of the *Viperfish* became so optimistic about trying again that I felt almost guilty when I left for California.

On my way to the airport to catch the flight to Los Angeles, I drove a rental car to Tripler Army Hospital to say good-by to Brian Lane. He was in the psychiatric ward of the hospital, the receptionist in the lobby said, in B Wing, with all the others having "that kind of a problem." As I hiked up to the third floor, I felt the same sense of anxiety that I had in the engine room at four hundred feet when Lane looked at me with that strange gaze and said, "You can't get to me."

After talking with a cluster of psychiatric nurses, I was directed far away from the severely disturbed patients in the B wing to the outside exercise area. Brian was in a fenced courtyard of the hospital grounds, an area that looked like a city park, complete with grass, benches, and trees. The compound was filled with Marines from Vietnam, wandering around under the trees, all wearing Tripler robes, most of them with shaved heads, which gave them a strange guru appearance. There were groups of rigidly calm Marines, with frozen expressions and vacant eyes, and other groups of agitated Marines, who were making rapid random movements with their arms or faces. The jolting thought hit me that some of these men might have been with me on my first flight to Hawaii, the ones I had sat with a thousand years ago before reporting to the *Viperfish*. I searched their faces as I looked for my shipmate, and I felt more of that same basic fear that I had felt on watch with him during our patrol.

"Hello, Roger." The familiar voice turned me in my tracks.

Brian's appearance shocked me, and I stepped back a pace. His skin was pale and covered with acne, his head shaved. A two-day beard darkened the lower half of his face. He was staring at me and smiling a half smile, his strange half smile that had been a part of the engine room during our last weeks at sea. Jesus Christ, Brian, I wanted to say, what have they done to you?

"Hello, Brian," I said. "How's it going?"

He studied me in silence for a couple of seconds too long and then looked down at his watch. "I'm okay," he answered in a drifting voice and continued to stare at his watch.

I tried to think of something appropriate to say while he concentrated on his watch. The puzzled expression on his face suggested that he was struggling with a basic thought process, perhaps trying to determine what the positions of the hands on the watch meant. He shook his wrist. He looked at me and then back at his watch again, and he finally fumbled with the band and removed the watch from his wrist.

"Are you sure you're okay?" I said, feeling my throat tighten and deciding to change the subject. "Everything's going fine on the boat."

My voice sounded strange to me. Everything's fine except that Chief Mathews has just left the *Viperfish* forever, I was thinking. He has just "non–volunteered" to nonsubmarine duty, and he has departed Pearl Harbor in a manner that suggests none of us will ever see him again. And you, Brian, are losing your mind.

Brian listened to his watch, studied it again, and becoming frustrated, looked like he was going to cry. His eyes appeared to have aged at least twenty years during the past two months as he lifted his face and stared at me.

"I can't understand anything any more, Roger," he said in a frightened voice. "Nothing makes any goddamn sense at all."

I said a few more words, tried to encourage him, and told him that we missed him on the boat and hoped that he would be okay. I mumbled, my words trailing off, my own thoughts becoming confused. We shook hands and said good–by, and I left him standing in the exercise yard, surrounded by the crowd of psychotic patients and holding his watch, while he tried to bring his mind back to the time before the *Viperfish*.

Burning rubber, I drove away from the hospital, my grip on the steering wheel a crushing force of anger. The rage followed me to the airport and, during the months ahead, clung to me like a curse, telling me without justification that I had in some way abandoned the man. I had not said the right things on watch when he was coming apart. I had driven off and left my shipmate helpless, in that company of psychotic men, with a mind that no longer worked as he struggled with a wristwatch that no longer made sense to him. I could not shake the feeling that I had left Brian in his time of greatest need.

My wedding and honeymoon with Keiko were something close to taking a brief but gigantic leap from the hell of Brian Lane's world straight up into heaven. As Keiko walked down the aisle of the USC Methodist chapel, she looked at me with the radiant happiness of a woman in love. Tears came to my eyes, and I was filled with her beauty. On our honeymoon to Canada, we explored every small town that we found along the way. I ignored newspapers and events of the world around us and shared the time, meant just for the two of us, only with Keiko. We returned to Honolulu with all of our belongings in one suitcase and one seabag and rented a small apartment in the little town of Waipio.

Before I reported back to the *Viperfish*, Keiko and I took an afternoon trip to the north shore of Oahu, where we could have a final picnic and I could do a little surfing. We had both become tense, the upcoming departure of the *Viperfish* continuously in our minds, and her burden had just been increased because her brother had received orders from the U.S. Army to report to Vietnam.

We spread our blanket on the coarse sand near the water, and she waited for me as I dragged my board into the ocean and paddled out to ride the waves. The surf was considerably bigger than usual because of a large swell pushing down from Alaska, and I moved far out to sea to reach the optimal point for takeoff. The vigorous exercise would be therapeutic, I had decided, and I felt that the greater amount of energy I expended, the easier the next two months under the ocean would be.

When I finally returned to shore, the sun had descended low on the horizon. Sunset Beach was beginning to move into darkness, and Keiko was no longer waiting on our blanket. I found her a couple of hundred yards away, standing at the water's edge, looking out into the ocean, and crying with the almost certain knowledge that I had drowned in the heavy surf.

Her look of relief at my appearance was quickly replaced by worry and anger.

"You're going out to sea in two days, and here I am thinking you have already drowned before even closing the hatch of that *thing*!" she said. Tears rolled down her face, her look of anguish reflecting the turmoil and fear inside. "It's not fair," she added in a small voice, the tears flowing freely.

I put my arm around her, and we gathered our belongings and drove back to our apartment. We talked late into the evening as I tried to explain why I had to leave, why it was so important, especially after what we had gone through so far. I talked and I talked, and when I finally ran out of steam, she looked at me and said, "But why are you going? Why don't they send someone else?"

I let her question hang in the air while my mind struggled for an answer. Looking at the whole matter objectively, she was right. Why would anybody in his right mind leave such a woman and such happiness and climb into a screaming engine room for two continuous months under the ocean?

The reason that I was going, I knew, was not just because I had been ordered to do so, although the military imperative certainly carried some weight. It was not to help discover whatever was out there because nobody would tell us what it was. I wasn't longing for glory–there certainly would be none–and I wasn't planning on receiving any thanks from my country because the American public no longer seemed to believe that military accomplishments were of any value.

"We are going," I finally said into the tropical night air, "because our mission has to be completed, and I trust the captain to get us there and back."

I could barely hear the soft words of her response, but she mentioned her brother in Vietnam, the men on the *Scorpion*, and the fact that trust might not be enough.

The next day, Chief Gary Linaweaver met us at a table near the row of submarines lining the pier at the Pearl Harbor submarine base. He talked solemnly to Keiko, his voice calm and comforting.

"Just remember," he said, "the *Viperfish* is nothing like the *Scorpion*. The *Scorpion* was a sleek fast–attack boat. She traveled fast and dove deep, she did the maneuvers those kinds of submarines do."

He smiled reassuringly. "The *Viperfish* is big and slow," he continued. "She doesn't move fast and she doesn't go deep. She just cruises along, staying pretty shallow, ready to surface immediately if there are any problems." He held his hands out, obviously without a worry in the world. "Your husband could not be on a safer ship!"

I was not sure how reassured Keiko was after that discussion, but she accepted his comments without question. She had not been told about the activities of our previous cruises. The mystery of the mission, coupled with the essence of submarine operations, gave all of the wives a burden that cannot be easily relieved, an ordeal that is shared by all who watch loved ones drive their submarines out to sea.

The separation of going to sea in this manner was more painful and more absolute than sheer time and distance could justify. The nature of the process itself, the submergence of the submarine, was an important factor in the loneliness of those left behind. For the wives on shore, watching their men disappear into the hatches, riveting their eyes on the silhouette of black steel as the boat moves to sea, and finally seeing the submarine vanish even before reaching the horizon can deliver a chilling fear into the heart of even the strongest person. This *disappearance* of the submarine, more than the departure, followed by a total absence of communications for weeks or months at a time, along with the secrecy of the mission and uncertainty of the submarine's location, render a daily torture for the women left behind.

Keiko drove me to the pier next to the *Viperfish* at midnight the night before we left. After sharing the greatest kiss of my entire life, I waved a final good–bye and climbed down the long ladder leading into the *Viperfish* engine room to prepare the submarine's nuclear reactor for the start–up.

Bringing a reactor to a power–producing state is a painfully exact procedure. With voltmeter and technical manuals at my side, I began testing all of the safety systems controlling the reactor. Start–up was planned for 0600 the next morning, which would allow Captain Harris to cast off the lines at exactly 0800.

Coffee became my salvation as the early hours of the morning slowly passed and daylight approached. Whenever I left the engine room to fill my cup in the crew's dining area, another crewman was coming on board. Each man appeared tired and anxious, as he sought a few hours' sleep before we were to push away from the submarine base.

"How's the start–up going, Dunham?" each man asked, and I said, "Perfect! The reactor comes on line at six and we're outa here by eight."

"Way to go, bruddah."

By 0300, the sleeping quarters were filled with the crew and the coffeepot was nearly empty. By 0400, I confirmed that the fission process would be safe; by 0500, I established that we would be able to conduct safe emergency shutdowns during the next two months if anything went wrong while the reactor was running.

By 0530, I had one final system to check before starting the reactor. Three large and powerful high–voltage circuit breakers had to be tested—one at a time. They had been previously tested and retested, so it was just a formality that I close the breakers one final time. The first two worked perfectly, but I quickly discovered that the third breaker was seriously damaged, its innards making the strange tinkling sound of pieces of metal falling apart. I looked at the clock—thirty minutes before start–up—and then glared at the breaker. The matter was simple enough: Without the breaker, we couldn't start the reactor; without the reactor, we couldn't go to sea.

Moving as quickly as possible, I turned off all electrical power to the system and tore the circuit breaker apart. I found a small strip of metal, no more than a half inch wide and two inches long, in three pieces instead of one.

There was no way to find a replacement part, not at 0530 or at 1000 that morning and probably not within the next week. The piece was uniquely *Viperfish,* and locating such parts sometimes took weeks and even months.

I looked around the engine room and tried to figure out what to do next.

Several minutes later, after I had broken every possible regulation that applied to the engine rooms of nuclear submarines, the circuit breaker worked perfectly. A Coca-Cola can, *minus* an identical metal strip a half inch wide and two inches long, landed in the dumpster at the side of the pier. At exactly 0600, the engine room filled with men as the reactor start-up neared completion. By 0800, the topside crew cast off our lines and we were on our way.

When Chief Linaweaver entered the engine room, I started to tell him the Coca-Cola story, but I hesitated and then changed the subject. No point in ruining the man's day, I decided. He definitely wouldn't SCRAM the reactor, turn off the electricity, and try to fix it himself, so there was no point in making him worry every time he looked at the circuit breaker during the next two months. I promised myself that I would find an official replacement part as soon as we returned to port. While the *Viperfish* headed down the channel in the direction of the Papa Hotel point that joined Pearl Harbor to the ocean, I mulled over just how far into outer space Admiral Rickover and every other design engineer would launch me if they ever heard of what I had used to keep one of our vital circuit breakers operational. And, for the next two months, every time I opened a can of Coca-Cola, I paused before taking a sip and thought about the No. 3 circuit breaker.

We cleared the entrance to Pearl Harbor at 0830 and promptly descended into the ocean. Our course was unknown, our speed was full power, and our destination was secret.

To the men in the engine room, our intent was clear. We had one last chance before the fuel was gone, and all of us felt a powerful determination to let nothing stop us. The pot–head students, the Vietnam War protests, the disruptions and turmoil of our society were all behind us now, and we found ourselves concentrating on the job ahead.

We ran out of real milk on the second day, and lettuce was gone by the fourth day. When we reached the Search Zone (as we began to call it), we were down to the usual canned, pickled, frozen, and otherwise preserved foods. Nobody was much interested in watching Regulus missile movies. If we crossed the 180th meridian into the Domain of the Golden Dragon, there was no announcement that we had done so. The machinery worked perfectly as our thundering propulsion turbines pushed us into colder waters. We finally slowed enough to allow for nearly silent operations for a couple of days as we made further progress through the ocean; about one week after departure, we reached our destination.

The civilians scrambled to line up the Fish with the hole at the bottom of the hangar. It was soon leaving the *Viperfish* and descending toward the ocean bottom, more than 15,000 feet below. To our surprise, we heard no detonations in the water. There was no need for emergency surfacing or sudden changes in depth. Hour upon hour, we slowly pulled our Fish through the water as it searched for a mystery lying somewhere far below.

In the engine room, I sat next to Donald Svedlow, both of us watching our panels and monitoring the various conditions that could shut down the nuclear plant or electrical systems. We didn't talk much about Brian Lane, and we didn't discuss the uncertain future of Paul Mathews. During the first few minutes of each four-hour watch, like a ritual, I lit up a cigar and Svedlow broke out a small can of chewing tobacco. As I filled the area with a cloud of smoke, he took a pinch of the stuff and jammed it into the corner of his mouth. We then sat back in our chairs and quietly watched the meters. To my considerable surprise, the reactor performed flawlessly week after week. We settled into a routine while we waited for an indication from the hangar compartment that something worthwhile was being accomplished. Between watches, I tried to read one of my several books, studied my cursed French lessons again, and, in the privacy of my rack, slowly thumbed through my stack of honeymoon pictures.

Every once in awhile, I downed a can of Coca-Cola and thought about circuit breakers.

After almost four weeks of searching, as our uranium fuel became further depleted, a new problem with the Fish equipment interrupted the flow of information from the bottom of the ocean. It was a fundamental design flaw in the winching system that prevented proper movement of the cable, a flaw that nobody could correct and one flaw that created a new level of frustration in the men working on the Fish. We could feel the contained rage of their failure. During meals, they talked little and poked at their food. Eventually, they dragged themselves back to the hangar to study the problem again and again.

By the fifth week, when the searching operation had come to a complete halt, morale dropped to the lowest level that I had seen since reporting on board.

At this point, Captain Harris turned the situation around for us in the form of a loudspeaker announcement, one of his rare broadcasts throughout the boat to all of us. I was calibrating a nuclear control circuit board at the far corner of the engine room when the speaker above my head came to life. I put down the equipment to listen.

"This is the captain speaking," the deep voice said, the words flowing with the authority of the commanding officer. "We have become hampered by equipment that was designed without benefit of practical experience. The Fish is now back inside the boat, and our search operation has been temporarily suspended. The flaws in this equipment must be corrected for us to complete our job."

I glanced down the passageway and noticed that the other men had also stopped their work to listen.

"We have come a long way during these past months," the captain continued, "but we have a considerable distance to go. The *Viperfish* has enough fuel for another four weeks, and we are going to remain here for that time as we work to find a solution. The equipment will not give us the answer. It is going to be up to the crew to find the answer." After outlining the details of our dilemma, he concluded the announcement by urging each of us to give our best effort.

Six hours later, as the captain sat in his stateroom and reviewed the design parameters of the winching system, a knock came at his door. Petty Officer Timothy Brown, one of the enlisted men working with the civilians in the hangar, was carrying several pieces of paper covered with penciled drawings. Brown was a big man with a gentle manner. His background was more mechanical than scientific, and he was known by the crew to be more of a worker than an innovator.

"Captain, I'm sorry to interrupt you," Brown said politely as he opened the door, "but I believe I have the solution to our problem."

Harris and Brown hunched over the tiny stateroom table for hours as they reviewed the sketches, criticized and analyzed the new concepts, and bounced fresh ideas back and forth within the cramped quarters.

"We drill a hole here," Brown said, his pencil racing across the drawing. "We insert a pin here; this will stabilize the bearing and prevent the movement of the shaft. And then we bolt this clamp here, like so."

The captain looked up at Brown, his bushy eyebrows drawn together with concern. "There are some pretty strong assumptions, here," he said.

"Yes, sir, there are," Brown answered, simply. "I did have to make some guesses, but I think it can work."

"It could conceivably stabilize the whole assembly," the captain agreed.

"It would take only a couple of days to do this, sir, all of us working together on this thing. There'll still be plenty of time left for the search."

Brown's design was accepted by the civilian scientists and incorporated into the winching system in less than two days. Soon after, everybody began the complex process of lowering the Fish through the hole. The cable moved freely with the revised winching mechanism, and the Fish again disappeared into the black ocean and moved along on its journey to the bottom nearly twenty thousand feet down.

Several days later, Robbie Teague prepared for another session in his darkroom on the port side of the hangar. During the time the Fish had been out of commission, his work had been minimal, with no pictures to analyze and nothing much to do but wait. When the Fish was brought back inside the *Viperfish* after the first run, Robbie finally had work to do.

Isolated within the confined darkroom on the port side of the hangar, he pulled film out of Fish canisters and applied chemicals until the 8 × 10 photographs provided testimony about the ocean floor. He kept the door tightly shut behind him as the glow of red light cast shadows over the trays filled with pictures. Bitter fumes from developer and fixer solutions burned his throat and lungs, flared his nostrils, and teared his eyes. The process of producing the stacks of photographs was tedious, and Robbie struggled to maintain a creative interest in the glossy pictures of mud.

Picture after picture looked the same. Each showed the flat expanse of sludge that had been only rarely interrupted by the drab outline of a sea cucumber. The strobe light on the Fish provided remarkably clear pictures, he noticed with some pride, and the stack of photos from this run was substantial.

Nobody had come around to tell Robbie what the pictures were supposed to show. His job was to take the pictures and review the results for clarity, focus, depth of field, and contrast. There was no reason for him to have any understanding about what might be at the bottom of the ocean. As the ship's photographer, he had no need to be included in the exclusive club of scientists and technicians involved in the operation of the Fish.

To Robbie, the past twelve hours had been just another routine photo session. Flipping through the stack of photographs, he saw mud in this one, more mud in the next one, and–look at that–a boulder here, and a little rock there. He reacted slightly at the next picture–a fish, a strange creature with wires coming out of its forehead, its huge eyes undoubtedly blinded from the power of the underwater strobe. He smiled at the thought of his job, studying mud and blinding creatures at the bottom of the Pacific Ocean. The Fish was about twenty feet above the floor, he guessed, as he turned to the next photograph.

Spanning the full length of the 8 × 10 glossy was the conning tower of a submarine.

Robbie froze, his hand tightening its grasp on the picture under the red light, his eyes scanning the details of the rough steel, his heart beginning an incessant pounding within his chest. He was immediately sure that it was not an American submarine. It resembled a Soviet boat. There were no sailplanes protruding from the side of the vessel, and it had four different periscope–like devices protruding from the top. The main section of the submarine, lying on its side, showed up in stark relief from the surrounding mud, and Robbie saw the fragmented edges of broken steel at the corner of the picture. The submarine's numbers had been painted over, and the superstructure appeared to have buckled from the stresses of its final descent.

Reaching for the telephone, he simultaneously grabbed the next picture. As he dialed the captain's stateroom, he saw the skeleton lying on the mud, thirty feet from the main structure.

"Captain here," the voice crackled into his ear.

"Captain Harris?" Robbie asked, his voice sounding strange.

"This is Captain Harris," the voice answered.

"Captain, this is Robbie Teague, up in the hangar–in the photo shack."

"Yes, go ahead."

"We have found what we are looking for."

The *Viperfish's* trip back to Pearl Harbor, three weeks later, was filled with an atmosphere of celebration. It was a matter of continuous amazement that nobody but the captain, the executive officer, and the ship's photographer knew what we were celebrating. A single announcement from the captain about our success had come over the loudspeakers. His voice was audibly shaky as he reported that we had found the object of our search. There were some further words of congratulations to every man of the *Viperfish* crew, and that was it.

A feast was served, banquet style, in the mess, and punchbowls were filled with juices having a special tang. The entire dining area displayed exceptional touches of culinary expertise that said "thank you" to all of us from the captain. I wandered back into the engine room, popped open a can of Coca-Cola in front of the circuit breakers, smiled, and felt good.

Long before we raised our periscope off the island of Kauai, channel fever struck and adrenaline surged through us as we moved closer to home. We had been at sea for two months, and the thought of getting back to the real world came to me with a blast of raw energy. Sleep was out of the question, watching movies or reading novels was impossible, and when I finally lined up the cross hairs of our periscope on the waterfalls, twenty miles away, I relished the beauty of the deep blue sky and the green mountains. Later that night, I crowded into the top of the sail with the lookouts and Lieutenant Pintard, where we all silently watched the soft beauty of our fluorescent wake and the distant lights of Honolulu under a spray of stars.

The next morning, the wives and other loved ones of the *Viperfish's* crew stood clustered together at the edge of the submarine pier and strained to see the first sign of the approaching boat. The day was warm and beautiful, with no signs of the quick squalls that were typical of the area. The past two months had been very long for all of them, and they were talking excitedly as they waited. Keiko wore a summer print dress and a wide-brimmed white hat. The other women displayed the full spectrum of colorful Hawaiian clothes.

Keiko had been called by Chief Linaweaver's wife the night before about the *Viperfish's* arrival time. This was part of an informal but extensive network system to notify all families of the boat's imminent arrival. Keiko had chased around to the super-markets and bought enough food for a royal feast to prepare for my homecoming.

"There it is!" Betty Linaweaver exclaimed, pointing across Pearl Harbor at the black shape of the *Viperfish* rounding the bend and heading toward the submarine base.

"Beautiful!" several women called at the same time as they admired the full Hawaiian lei, wrapped around the sail, that extended almost all the way to the deck.

"What is that thing at the top of its periscope?" one of the children asked as the *Viperfish* glided across the water and moved closer to the submarine pier.

"It's a lei," the child's mother said. "A welcoming boat carries it out to them as they're coming up the channel—"

"Not *that*," the child said. "That *other* thing, sticking straight up."

"I don't know," another woman called out, peering at the periscope. "It looks like a stick or something is attached—"

"It's a broom!" another woman exclaimed.

Keiko turned, puzzled, to the woman standing next to her. "A broom?" she asked.

The chief of the boat ordered the *Viperfish*'s crew to secure from the maneuvering watch after our lines were attached to the pier. I deactivated the circuit breakers and handed an astounded Chief Linaweaver an official supply request for a new Mod 1, Mark 2, strip of metal. Finally, climbing up the ladder leading out of the engine room, I blinked at the brilliant tropical sunlight that I hadn't seen for two months and turned toward the pier. I immediately spotted Keiko waving frantically to me, her face lit up with happiness.

About five enthusiastic minutes later, she diplomatically mentioned that I smelled sort of...funny.

"Funny?" I asked. "I showered twice, I even took an extra long shower so I'd really smell good. I used a lot of soap, too."

She smiled. "Maybe it just doesn't come off."

"Maybe what doesn't come off?"

"That smell, whatever it is." She smiled and kissed me again. "It's not a bad smell," she said, "it's kind of a...submarine smell. Like diesel oil or machinery, or something."

"Well, I'll shower again when—"

She touched her finger against my lips. "No," she said softly, "*we'll* shower when we get home. And don't plan on much sleep tonight."

Holding her tightly against me, I felt her warmth and the final relief from the aching separation that we had both experienced.

Thirty feet from where we stood, three naval officers with more gold on their uniforms than I had ever seen climbed out of an official black U.S. Navy limousine. They stood near the side of the car and quietly watched the men walking across the brow. Captain Harris and Lieutenant Dobkin were the last to come through the control room hatch and appear on the deck of the boat. They were immediately joined by two armed guards from the submarine base. As the guards escorted the men across the brow toward the pier, I noticed that Dobkin was carrying a black briefcase with heavy locks attached to the top. The case was big enough to hold hundreds of glossy photographs, and a large pair of steel handcuffs secured the handle of the briefcase to his left wrist. The men climbed into the limousine, and it sped away.

Keiko and I walked down the pier to our car, hand in hand. She told me that she had seen the broom and knew that we had been successful.

"I can't say anything—" I started to say, when she interrupted me.

"You don't have to say anything at all, honey," she said softly as our hands tightened. "I'm proud of you, I'm glad you're back safely, and I love you."

We drove away from the pier and the *Viperfish*, turned left on Kamehameha Highway, and rushed past the vast fields of sugar cane to the quiet little apartment waiting for us in the hills of Oahu.

EPILOGUE

SEPTEMBER 1968. At a secret ceremony on the Pearl Harbor Submarine Base, Capt. Thomas Harris received the Distinguished Service Medal, one of the highest honors awarded by the U.S. Navy. This was the first time since 1914 that an officer of his rank had received such a commendation, and an appropriate notation was made in his service record.

AT A REMOTE CORNER of Pearl Harbor Submarine Base, on the deck of the USS *Viperfish*, a high-ranking entourage, on behalf of President Lyndon B. Johnson, sequestered the crew for a special ceremony. Unlike all other such ceremonies, there was no announcement of the event, and the uniform of the day was dungarees. Ribbons were handed to each man, and an admiral read a quick message:

> The President of the United States takes pleasure in presenting the Presidential Unit Citation to the crew of the USS [*Viperfish* (SSN-655)], for service as set forth in the following citation:

215

For exceptionally meritorious service in support of National Research and Development efforts while serving as a unit of the Submarine Force, United States Pacific Fleet. Conducting highly technical submarine operations, over an extended period of time, the USS [Viperfish (SSN-655)] successfully concluded several missions of significant scientific value to the Government of the United States. The professional, military, and technical competence, and the inspiring devotion to duty of [Viperfish] officers and men, reflect great credit upon themselves and the United States Naval Service.

Lyndon B. Johnson

JANUARY 1969. The official black Navy limousine approached the Marine guard gate at the end of the long bridge connecting the city of Vallejo to the nuclear submarine shipyard on Mare Island, California. Slowing near the guard, the driver rolled down his window and briskly returned the Marine's salute.

"May I see your identification, sir?" the guard asked the white-haired man in the back seat.

"This is Admiral Hyman G. Rickover," the driver said authoritatively.

"Thank you, sir," the guard answered the driver, looking again at the man in the back seat. "May I see your identification, sir?"

The guard knew exactly who the man was; all the guards had known he was coming for days. And if there ever was a time to follow orders precisely to the letter, this was it.

The back door opened. Looking furious, the white-haired man jumped out. He moved around the guard and started marching down the street in the direction of Mare Island.

"Sir, you must show your identification!" the guard called, his right hand nervously fingering the top of his pistol.

The man continued walking as the driver and the other passenger in the limousine flashed their identification cards and moved forward to pick up the man. The Marine guard raced to the nearby Marine Corps office, ordered a relief guard in his place, and mustered five more men. They all jumped into a military pickup truck and chased behind the limousine, across the bridge and across Mare Island in the direction of the USS *Viperfish*.

While Captain Harris waited in the wardroom, I stood the reactor shutdown watch in the engine room of the boat. We were both awaiting Admiral Rickover's arrival. We had known he was coming, and everybody had worked to ensure that the engine room was in perfect condition for his inspection. Alone in the maneuvering area, I paced back and forth and watched the meters while waiting for the baggy pants to show at the top of the engine-room hatch.

"He's coming!" Seaman Gerard Snyder called down from his station on the topside deck of the *Viperfish*. "A black limousine and a pickup truck filled with Marines!"

Pacing more vigorously, I wondered if the admiral was going to bring some of his NR men and suddenly remembered the Rickover-inspired purges on other boats.

The limousine, still followed by the Marines, screeched to a halt at the pier next to the *Viperfish*, and everybody climbed out. On board the *Viperfish*, Snyder quickly checked his uniform and nervously patted his .45-caliber pistol at his side.

"Request permission to come aboard!" one of the NR men in a dark blue officer's uniform called out as three men moved across the brow.

Snyder saluted the group and replied, "May I see your identification, sir?"

The officer turned and pointed to the white-haired man. "This is Admiral Hyman G. Rickover!"

"Attention on deck!" Snyder hollered as everybody standing nearby saluted the men again. "May I see some identification, sir?" he repeated.

As the men glared at Snyder, the young submariner suddenly brightened. They were testing him, that had to be the answer. They wanted to see if he would remember to check the shipyard access list. The admiral certainly would be on the access list.

"Would you like me to check for the admiral's name on the access list, sir?" Snyder asked.

The men became further enraged as they turned and stormed off the *Viperfish*. Snyder looked down at the access list and wondered if he had said something wrong. Shortly after the limousine screeched a streak of rubber down the pier, Snyder called me in the engine room.

"He's gone!"

"Gone?" I said into the telephone. "Admiral Rickover is gone?"

"He's gone and so are the Marines!"

Several minutes later, after a call to the *Viperfish*, Captain Harris left the boat and crossed Mare Island to the U.S. Naval Headquarters office. As he walked into the room, Admiral Rickover was waiting.

"You do not want me down on your boat?" the admiral demanded. "Are you still keeping some of those goddamn deep-submergence secrets you didn't want to tell me last year?"

"Of course, you may come aboard our–"

"And you are two goddamn weeks behind in refueling the reactor!"

"You know about that, Admiral," Harris said, trying to keep a calm voice. "The shipyard lost the tip of a glove into the –"

"The refueling is not on goddamn schedule!"

"I'm not sure you are getting accurate information, Admiral, and–"

"Enough, Harris, I don't want to see your goddamn boat! You are relieved of command, and your next fitness report will reflect the reason for this action."

As a result of the admiral's concluding sentence and events that followed, the distinguished career of Comdr. Thomas Harris was brought to an end by Adm. Hyman G. Rickover. There was no appeal, and no man in the Submarine Service would risk his own career by challenging the final decision of such an authority.

*   *   *

1 NOVEMBER 1969.

Dear Mr. Dunham:

I recall the mission of the USS [*Viperfish*], and I have checked into your record of service in the Navy.

Knowing what I do of the extremely demanding test you met on the [*Viperfish*], I have no hesitation in commending you to any school to which you apply, as meeting the highest tests of character and responsibility.

You are free to use this letter in your applications for medical school.

I hope and expect that you will go forward in your career in civil life with the same distinction you exhibited in the years you served your country.

Sincerely,
President Lyndon B. Johnson
Austin, Texas

5 MAY 1972. Warrant Officer Robbie Teague, Special Project photographer on board the USS *Viperfish,* was killed in an automobile accident on a Maryland State Highway. He was buried with honors at the Arlington National Cemetery, Fort Meyer Army Base, Arlington, Virginia.

30 APRIL 1975. After the United States Congress rejected President Gerald Ford's request for further supplemental aid to continue the Vietnam War, South Vietnam President Nguyen Van Thieu resigned and fled the country. As the remaining Americans were evacuated from the roof of the U.S. embassy in Saigon, acting President Duong Van Minh surrendered unconditionally to the North Vietnamese, ending the Vietnam War.

30 JUNE 1976. At Mare Island Naval Shipyard, Vallejo, California, the USS *Viperfish* was decommissioned following a brief ceremony at the pier alongside the submarine. Several men from her former patrols attended the emotional event and spoke eloquently of her past. Her Special Projects equipment and nuclear reactor core were removed; the large hole at the base of the vessel's hangar compartment was permanently sealed shut. She was finally delivered to the mothball fleet in Bremerton, Washington, after efforts to scuttle the submarine were abandoned.

On 1 September 1994, the hull of the empty submarine was cut up and the pieces melted down into steel ingots for distribution to recycling plants throughout the United States.

At regular five-year intervals, the men of the spy submarine *Viperfish* gather together to remember the days gone past and to pay tribute to their shipmates who have "rested their oars" and sailed on to their eternal patrol.

SOURCES

Most of the information gathered for this story originated from sources that cannot be revealed. The highly classified nature of the *Viperfish* mission and the sensitivity of events relating to such U.S. submarine operations prevent discussion of additional specifics. All official requests for information through the Freedom of Information Act were denied, as were all appeals of such denials.

The following unclassified sources provided historical and technical information for this story.

Birtles, Philip, and Paul Beaver. *Missile Systems.* Runnymede, England: Ian Allan Ltd., 1985.

Blackman, Raymond V. B. *Jane's Book of Fighting Ships.* New York: McGraw–Hill, 1966, 1967, 1968.

Bussert, Jim. "The Safety of Soviet Nuclear Submarines." *Jane's Defence Weekly,* 18 April 1987, 715.

Calvert, James F. "Up Through the Ice of the North Pole." *National Geographic* 126 (July 1959): 1.

Clancy, Tom. *Submarine.* New York: Berkeley Publishing Group, 1993.

Cousteau, Jacques-Yves. *The Ocean World of Jacques Cousteau. Volume 1: Oasis in Space.* N.p.: Danbury Press, 1973.

Decommissioning Ceremony. Mare Island, Calif.: Mare Island Naval Shipyard, 1976. Booklet.

Department of Defense. *Soviet Military Power 1984.* Washington, D.C.: Government Printing Office, 1984.

Dornik, William, Roy Armstrong, Dan Simmons, and Phillip Thomas. "Crew Reunion." Private publication for 1991 reunion of [*Viperfish*] crew.

Friedman, Norman. *U.S. Submarines since 1945: An Illustrated Design History.* Annapolis, Md.: Naval Institute Press, 1994.

Gunston, Bill. *Submarines in Color.* New York: Arco Publishing Company, 1977.

National Geographic Society. World Ocean Floors, Pacific Ocean. Map. Washington, D.C.: National Geographic Society, June 1992.

The Navy's Nuclear Field. U.S. Navy recruiting booklet, 1 September 1981.

Nuclear Field. U.S. Navy recruiting booklet, 1 March 1985.

Prokhorov, A. M. *Great Soviet Encyclopedia.* 3d ed. Vol. 5. New York: Macmillan, 1970.

Sobel, Lester A. *Facts on File Yearbook.* New York: Facts on File, 1966–68.

ABOUT THE AUTHOR

Roger C. Dunham, M.D., served in the Submarine Service as a nuclear reactor operator during the 1960s. Following honorable discharge from the U.S. Navy in 1969, he attended the University of Southern California, where he was elected president of the Premedical Honor Society. He graduated from the University of California, Los Angeles, School of Medicine in 1975.

Dr. Dunham practices full time as a board–certified specialist in internal medicine. He has served as chief of staff of a Southern California medical center for eight years and is currently the medical director of a multispecialty health care system. He is the author of two medical thrillers, *Final Diagnosis* and *The Anthrax Diagnosis*, and a screenplay, *The Diagnosis*.

Dr. Dunham and his wife, Keiko, have been married for twenty–eight years and have two children, Rochelle and Stephen.